Oracle VirtualBox Administration

ARUN KUMAR

Oracle VirtualBox Administration

Copyright © 2019 by Arun Kumar

Founder and Instructor at DBA Genesis

```
Note: All the queries in this book will look like
this format.
```

For any queries, write to support@dbagenesis.com

DEDICATION

I would like to dedicate this book to my family, who has been always there for me whenever I need

ACKNOWLEDGEMENT

Your comments encourage us to produce quality content, please take a second and say 'Hi' to me and let me and my team know what you thought of the book … p.s. It would mean the world to me if you send a quick email to me ;)

Email: support@dbagenesis.com

- Link to full course: https://dbagenesis.com/
- Link to all DBA courses: https://dbagenesis.com/courses
- Link to real-time projects: https://dbagenesis.com/p/projects
- Link to support articles: https://support.dbagenesis.com

All the best and I hope you enjoy this book!

Arun Kumar

Table of Content

## CHAPTER 1

Be Comfortable with Virtualization

Why virtualization

In this lesson, we will discuss about Virtualization.

Virtualization is running multiple operating systems or running a different operating system on top of an existing operating system.

For example: Suppose you have a laptop and you are running a windows operating system. Now you want to practice Linux on your system. Then you need to install Virtualization software and using this software, you install the Linux on top of the windows operating system.

There are actually two ways to do it.

First one is the hard way where you remove the Windows operating system and install the Linux on your system. The problem with this way is that you can only use Linux now.

The other way is Virtualization where you install Linux on top of the Windows which makes you use both the operating systems on the same system.

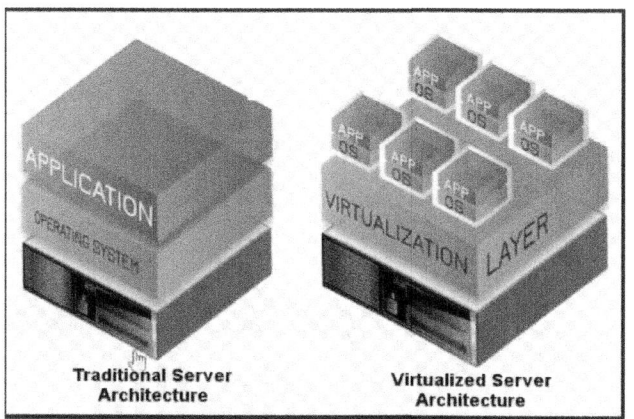

Traditional Server
Architecture

Virtualized Server
Architecture

The above picture shows the Traditional Server Architecture and the Virtualized Server Architecture.

In the Traditional Server, we have the server at the lowest point. In the server, we have the Operating system and on the top of the operating system, we have the Application.

The problem with traditional server architecture is it generally uses only 40 percent of your hardware capacity with only one operating system. So the 60 percent is wasted.

Virtualization actually helps the system to increase the hardware utilization capacity.

In the second picture of Virtualized server Architecture, the lowest point is the hardware or the server. Instead of one single operating system, we can install a virtualization software.

The benefit of the virtualization software is that we can install multiple operating systems and each operating system can have its own applications.

So in this way, the hardware capacity is fully utilized under Virtualization.

There are many types of Virtualization. Some types are mentioned below:

- Software virtualization
- Memory virtualization
- Storage virtualization
- Data virtualization
- Network virtualization

So we can also have the definition of Virtualization as:

Having a virtual setup of something which is not directly running on a physical layer is Virtualization

Example: Suppose you have one physical network but virtually you have created more IP addresses on the same physical network. This is called Network virtualization.

Virtualization vendors in market

In this lesson, we will be discussing about the different virtualization vendors in the market.

If you search in Google for virtualization software, you will get many vendors who provide the virtualization software such as VMware vSphere, Microsoft virtual server, Xen server, Docker and many more.

You will use this virtualization software in order to create more machines on your system and each machine is again dedicated to one operating system. So, each machine will have its own operating system, RAM, hard disk and that machine will be isolated from the other machines.

We have two types of products in virtualization platforms:

- **OS based virtualization:** You will have the product which will be installed on another operating system. It can be Windows or Linux operating system working as a base OS. We generally install VMware workstation or Oracle VirtualBox and then we can create virtual machines over it. These kinds of virtualizations are done to practice at home or for small level virtualizations.

- **ESXI software based virtualization:** In the real world or in a bigger picture, we use ESXI. **EXSI is an operating system**

in itself. So you do not need any separate operating system to work as a base OS. You just install the EXSI software on a server and directly start creating virtual machines.

So if the virtualization is for a normal testing purpose, you can install VMware or VirtualBox on the existing operating system on a small server and create the VM machines and do the testing. You can complete it on a small setup.

But if you are going for a full scale virtualization platform, you actually need to get an ESXI operating system. **When you install ESXI software, you do not need to again install VMware workstation or oracle VirtualBox on top of ESXI because the OS itself is virtualization software.**

In windows, you can create files and folders. In the same way, you can create virtual machines in ESXI.

We will be using Oracle virtual box in our eBooks and courses. You can also download it as is free of cost and does not require any license. For other products in the market like VMware, you need to take the license.

How to find if your system supports virtualization

Are you interested in Virtual Machines, Virtualization, Hypervisor, whatever name you call it and not sure if your Windows box supports Intel VT-x or AMD-V? This post tells you how to find out for yourself.

But, first the big question:

Do you need Intel VT-x or AMD-V based CPU to run Virtual Machines?

The answer is both Yes and No. Intel VT-x or AMD-V capable processors have inbuilt set of processor instruction that can handle virtualization effectively. To be able to use these instructions, they need to be enabled in BIOS. By default they are not enabled. Some say that enabling virtualization in BIOS slows down the performance of the CPU. But these days, the lag is hardly noticeable. My experience is that, enabling Inter VT or AMD-V did not slow down the performance of my computer.

So to give it to you straight, If you plan to run 64 bit virtual machines on your computer, you need a Intel VT-x or AMD-V.. But if you plan to run 32 bit virtual operating system as guest, you don't need Intel VT-x or AMDV CPU. Any normal CPU would work just fine.

How to check if your CPU has Intel VT-x or AMD-V?

You need to check for Intel VT-x if you are using Intel based CPU and AMD-V if you are using AMD CPU. They are the same technology offered by two different processor manufacturers.

You can check if your CPU has virtualization technology or not right from within Windows OS. All you have to do is to boot your computer if you have not done it already and follow any of the below methods.

Easiest option- Check your Task Manager

If you have Windows 10 or Windows 8 operating system, the easiest way to check is by opening up Task Manager->Performance Tab. You should see Virtualization as shown in the below screenshot. If it is enabled, it means that your CPU supports Virtualization and is currently enabled in BIOS. If it shows disabled, you need to enable it in BIOS. If you don't see virtualization, it means that your CPU does not support virtualization.

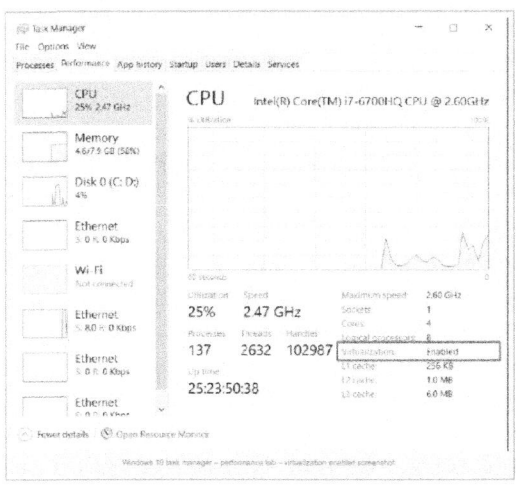

How to enable virtualization at BIOS level

How to Enable Intel VT-x in BIOS?

BIOS acronym for Basic Input/Output System is a firmware which is stored in a ROM (read Only Memory) chip on the motherboard. BIOS has a set of instructions that allows the computer to boot correctly. It is also used to initialize the hardware such as keyboard, HDD, processor, etc...

Step 1- Enter BIOS setup utility

BIOS has a setup utility that allows you to set or unset a particular property. For example, most common is to boot from CD ROM first which in most of the cases is set to boot from HDD (Hard Drive).

You cannot enter BIOS Utility when you have already booted into windows or Linux OS. You will have to restart your computer and there are is a combination of key strokes that you will have to press after the computer powers on but before it begins to boot from HDD or CD ROM. You will have to be very quick after you power on your computer, else, the computer will begin to boot from HDD. In that case, shout down or restart your system and try again.

Unfortunately, every motherboard manufacturer or laptop manufacturer will have a different key combination of entering into BIOS Utility. This you will have to find out by searching Google and typing Keywords like How to enter BIOS in MSI. Here instead of MSI, it could be Sony, HP, Lenovo etc.. based on your laptop or desktop. Then ready through a couple of suggested pages and you will get the answer.

Step 2- Change Virtualization Technology from Disabled to Enable

After you have entered BIOS setup Utility, using the arrow keys, look for Virtualization Technology which should mostly likely be in System Configuration Tab or Advanced Chipset settings. This will change depending on the manufacturer. In any case look for Virtualization Technology. Use the arrow keys to Change from Disable to Enable. You then have to save and exit. In most of the cases, you will have to press F10 to save and exit. But it can vary. Look at the bottom of the BIOS Utility screen, you will see the key which saves and exists.

That's it. You are done. VT is enabled.

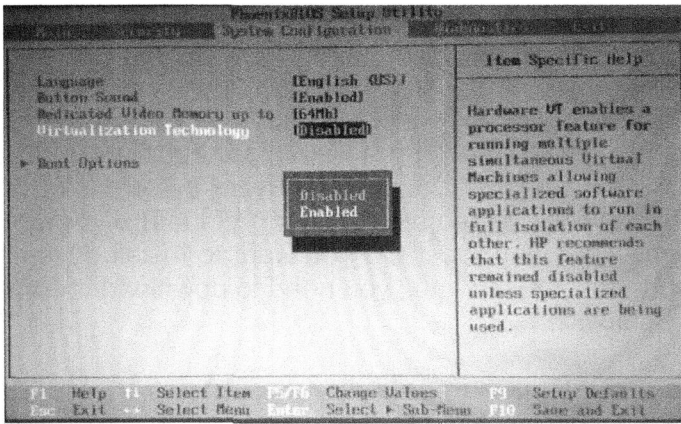

Download and install Oracle Virtual Box

Let us download the VirtualBox. The URL for the VirtualBox is available in the webpage below:

Download

Download and Install VirtualBox on win10.pdf

https://www.virtualbox.org/wiki/Downloads

You can directly copy and paste the URL and download link. You will see the page as below:

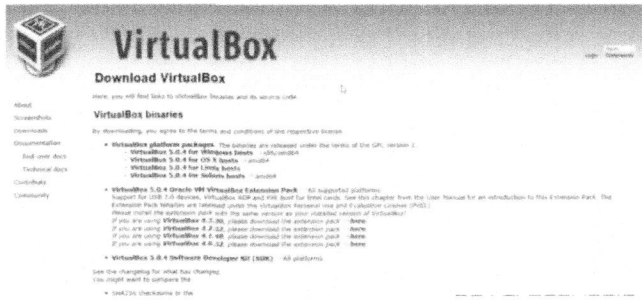

In the above link, you need to download the VirtualBox depending on the host operating system or the OS on which you are going to install the VirtualBox.

People get confused on what is host and what is guest.

Suppose you need to learn Linux or you want to install Linux on VirtualBox, you will think that you need to download VirtualBox for Linux hosts. This is a wrong assumption. You need to download the VirtualBox for the host OS. Suppose your system is having host OS as windows, you need to download the VirtualBox for windows hosts irrespective of what guest OS you want to install or run afterwards. So, if your host OS is Linux, you need to download the VirtualBox for Linux hosts.

So, the VirtualBox compatibility should match with the host OS but not with the guest OS.

I will choose the option which is VirtualBox for Windows hosts as my system is having windows.

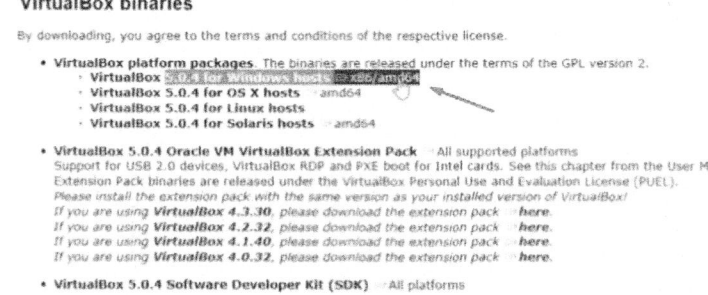

Click on the link and the download will start. Once the download is complete, run the installer. Let us look at all the installation screens:

Click on Next and a new screen will come

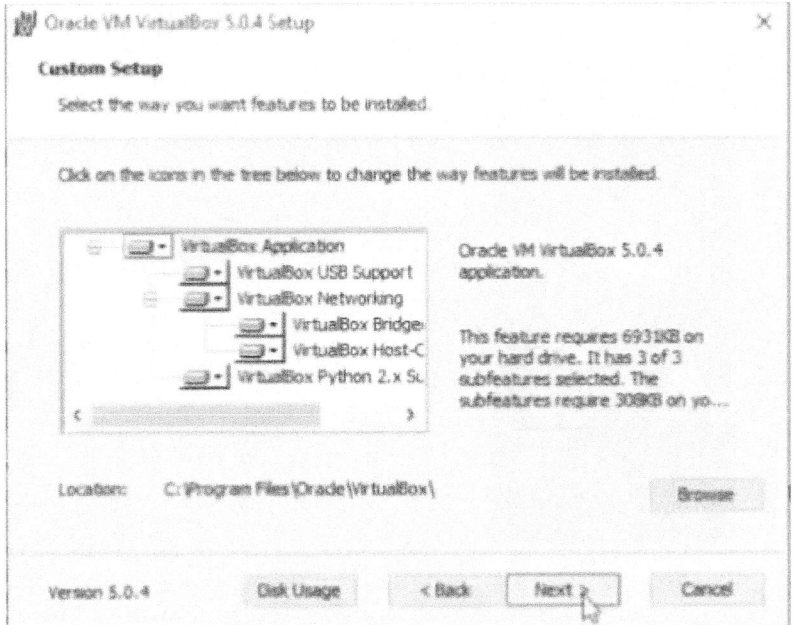

Click on Next, a new screen will appear

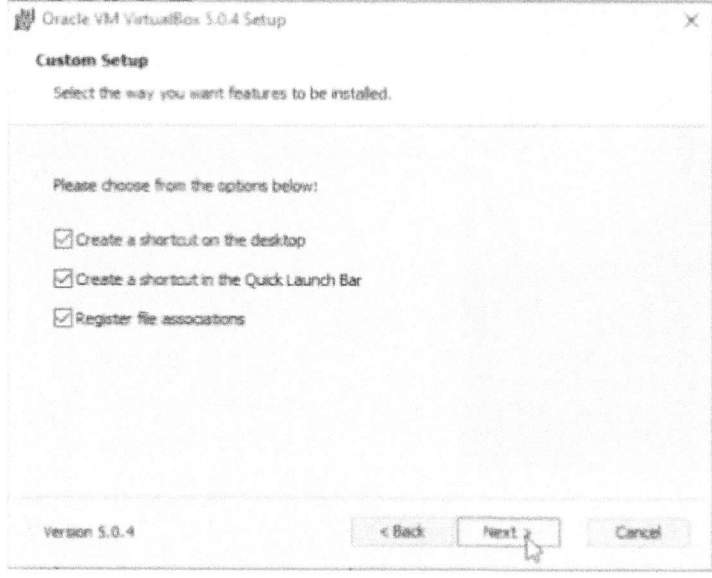

Click on Next, a new screen will appear

Click on Yes and the new screen will come asking you to finish the setup.

When you click on Finish, it will start the installation. Once the installation is complete, you will get a shortcut on your desktop.

Navigating Virtual Box

When you install the VirtualBox and start it from your desktop, the below screen will appear which is the first screen of the VirtualBox.

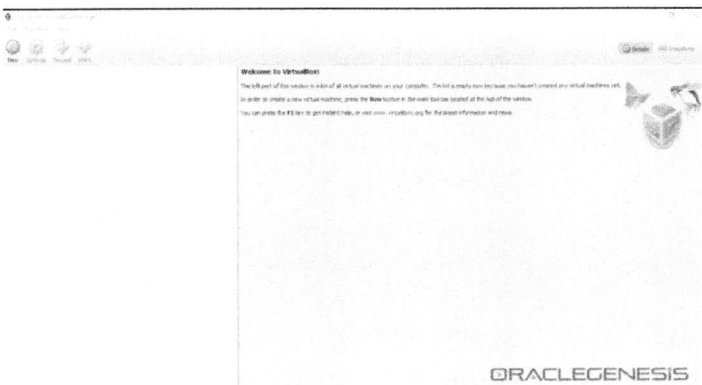

So basically, VirtualBox is a very simple and sweet virtualization platform. It has a very simple yet very powerful interface.

We will look into the tabs of the first screen of VirtualBox.

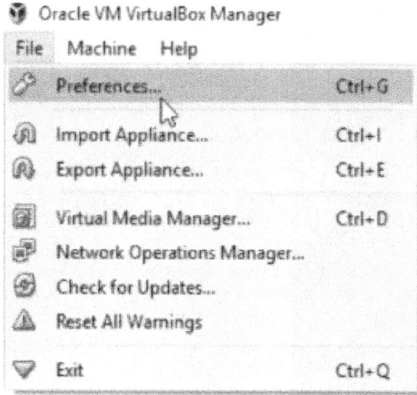

In the above picture, you can see the option **Preferences** under **File tab.**

With this option, you can set a path where you want to save your virtual machines that you create. So you can allocate one specific area in your hard drive for all the new virtual machines. Likewise we select a few preferences under this option.

Then we will look into the option **Export Appliance.**

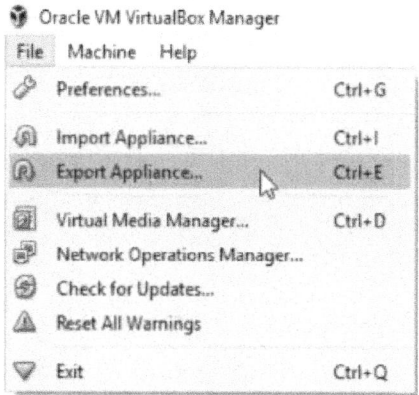

Suppose you have created one virtual machine and you want to share it with your friend. You can export that virtual machine using the option Export Appliance.

Also the option **Import Appliance** will come into the picture when you want to import some virtual machine. Let us say you have shared one virtual machine using Export Appliance. Now your friend will use the option Import Appliance and import that virtual machine.

The other options in the File tab are:

Virtual Media Manager - It is the central manager for all the hard disk, cd drives and floppy drives. These are the drives that will be virtually used in your VirtualBox.

Network Operations Manager - This is the option where you can play around the network of your VirtualBox.

The next tab is Machine.

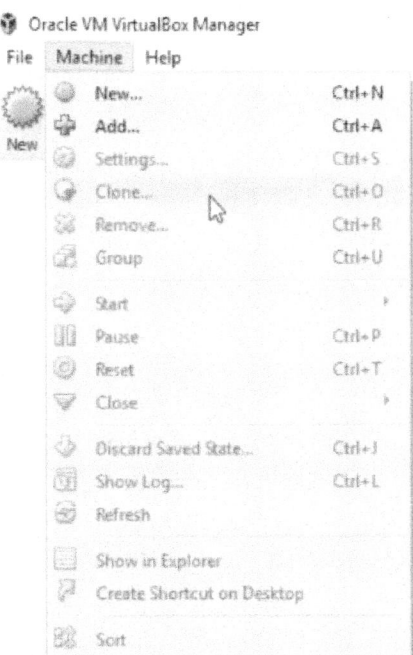

When you create a new virtual machine, it gets listed in the white panel or space just below the tabs (file, machine, help). When you highlight a virtual machine from the list of all the virtual machines listed, all the options under Machine tab will be available for you. For example: you can start a machine using Start option, you can pause it using Pause option, you can reset it using Reset and so on.

The last tab is **Help** which is nothing but the VirtualBox help center.

## CHAPTER 2

Prepare your First Virtual Machine

Create First Blank Machine

Now we will learn how to create a blank virtual machine.

Basically when you create a virtual machine, you need to create a blank machine first and then you install an operating system into the blank virtual machine.

So first we will understand **how to create a blank virtual machine** without any OS in it.

Click on New option, a window will open

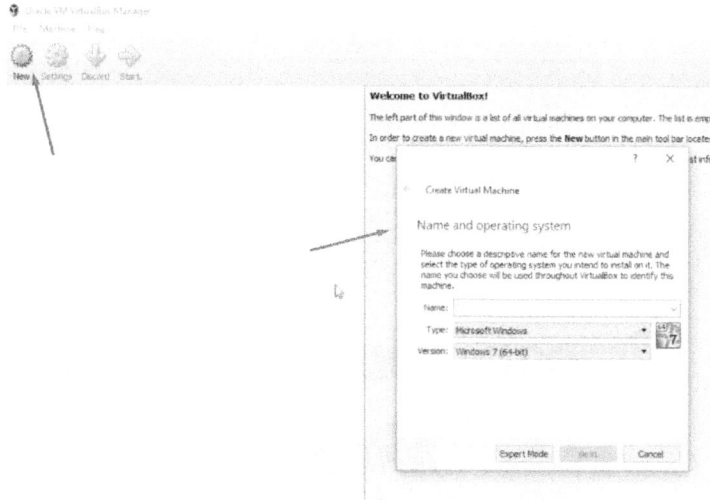

You need to give a name to your virtual machine. You can also choose the type of operating system that you want to install in it and you can even choose the version.

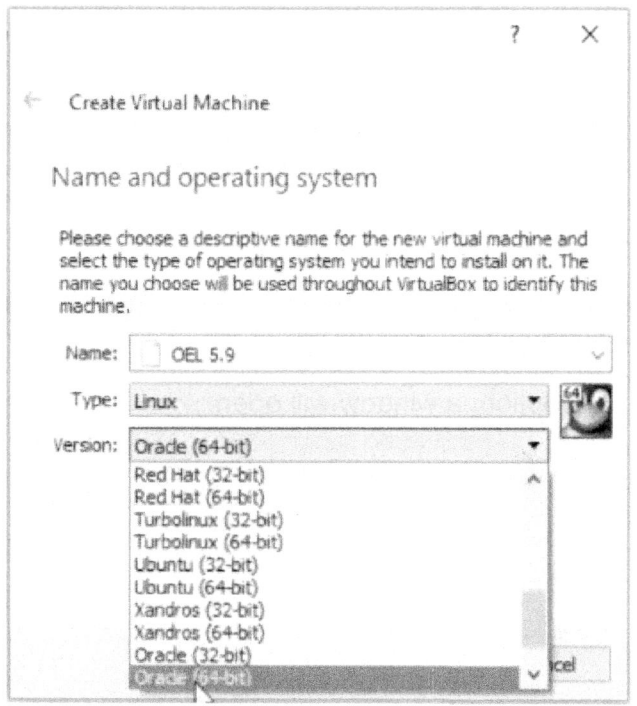

I named the virtual machine as OEL 5.9 and chose the OS type as Linux and the version as Oracle 64 bit. You can give a name of your choice and you can choose the operating system from the drop down menu in "Type" and you can choose the version also from the drop down menu in "Version".

Then click on Next

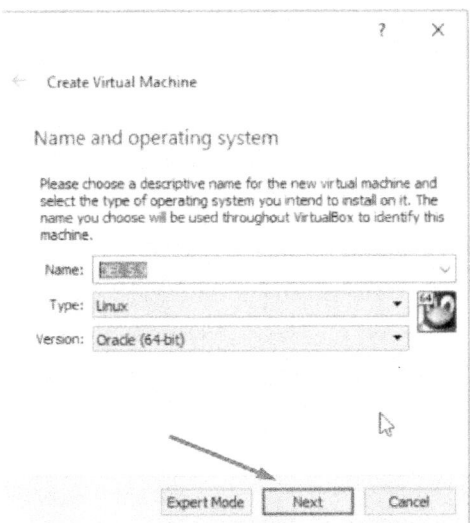

After clicking on Next, a new screen will open asking for the RAM size

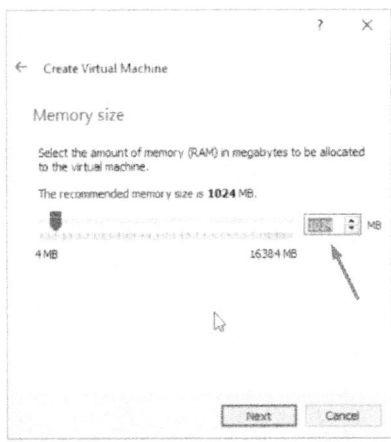

You can allocate anything depending on the size of your physical system. In the above screenshot, the total physical RAM is around 16GB. You need to follow the course requirement and allocate the RAM size according to the course that you take. I recommend you to go with 4GB of RAM.

When you are done selecting the RAM size, click on Next. A new screen will open which will ask you to assign a Hard disk.

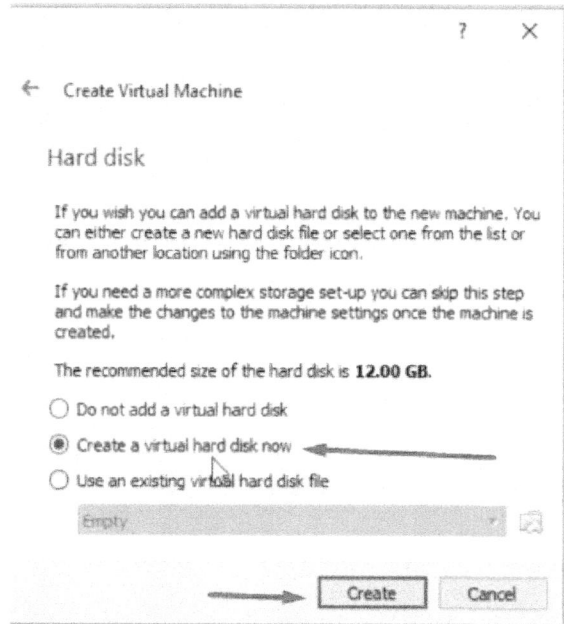

We will choose the default option already selected in the list - "Create a virtual hard disk now"

Then we will click on Create

A new screen will come asking you the Hard disk file type. You will go for the default one which is VDI (VirtualBox Disk Image).

Then click on Next.

It will ask you to choose the option whether the Hard disk size should be fixed in future or it should increase.

You will go for the option Dynamically allocated

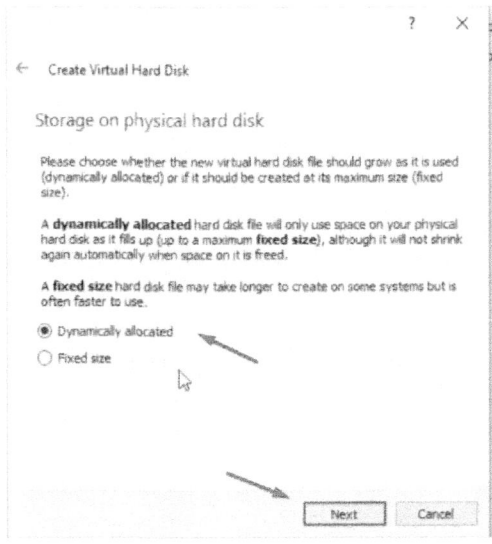

Now after clicking Next, it will ask for the Size of the hard disk. Normally for only Linux, you require about 20GB but it is recommended as a standard that you go for 50GB for the initial setup. It is good to have that much space when you play around and practice more and more.

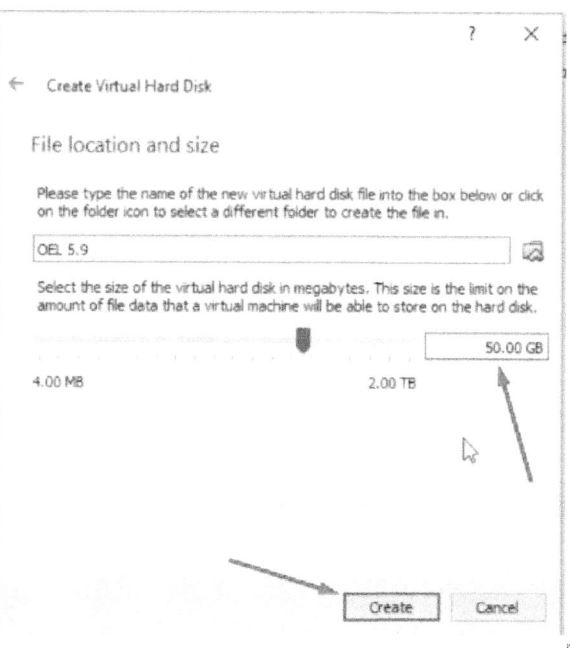

Then you need to choose Create and a blank virtual machine will be created.

So we have created a blank virtual machine. The name of the machine is OEL 5.9 and its status is Powered off as shown on the Left-hand side of the screen.

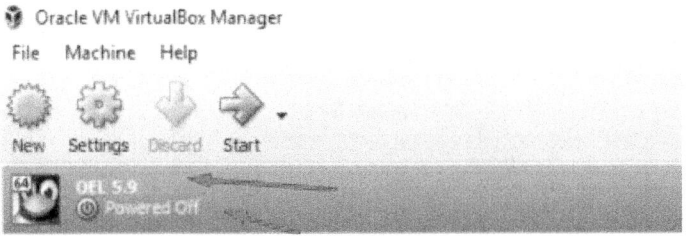

On the right hand side of the screen, you will have all the components of the virtual machine.

We will have the name and the Operating system which is not yet installed in the machine. We have just instructed or told the virtual machine that we will install the Oracle (64 bit) into it.

Suppose we want to create another virtual machine, you just have to follow the same steps mentioned above and the new virtual machine will be ready in the list below the first one in the white panel or space (left hand side).

As discussed earlier, you need to highlight the virtual machine on which you are working from the list and go to the Machine tab from the top menu. You can access the settings related to your highlighted virtual machine.

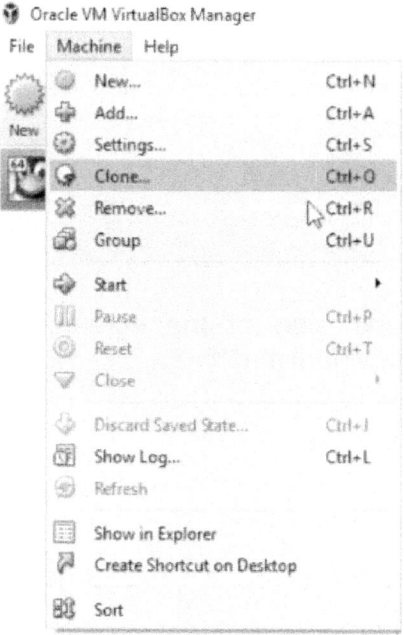

You can also access the settings by clicking on the settings tab just beside the New tab.

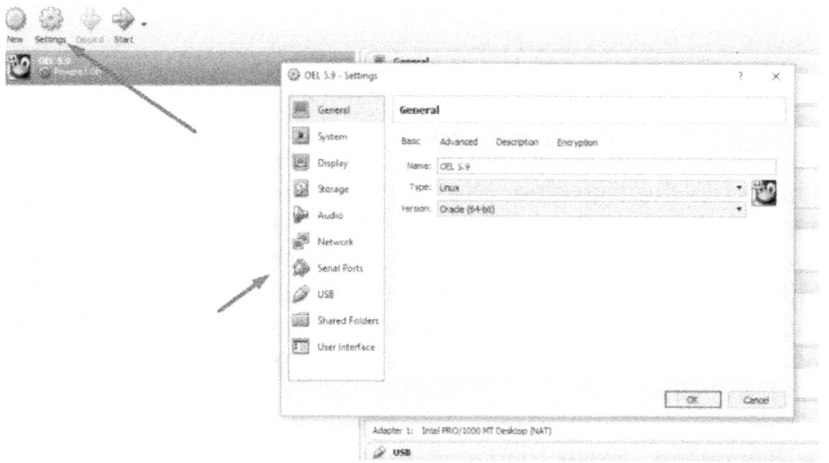

Also the options that you get by clicking on the Machine tab, the same options you can also get by right clicking on the virtual machine.

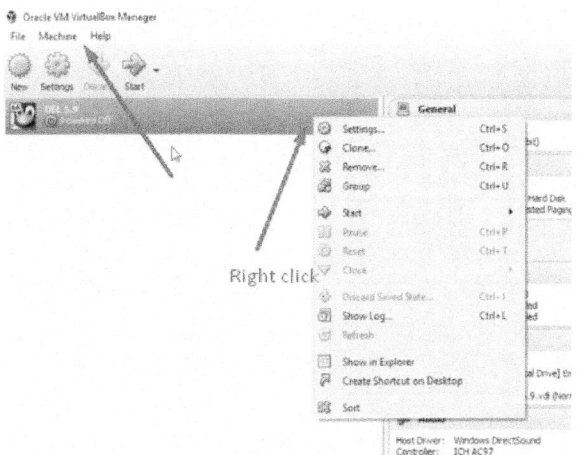

Decide IP Address for Your Virtual Machine

Before we start installing Oracle Enterprise Linux (OEL) on our blank virtual machine, we need to decide what IP address we should assign to our blank virtual machine.

First we will open the command prompt of our windows if Windows is our host operating system. Then we will type "ip config"

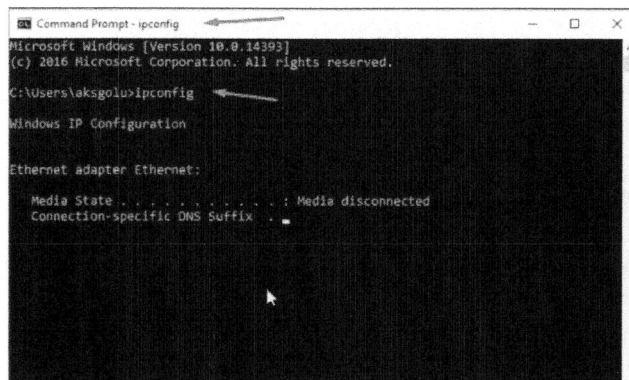

This will give you all the IP configuration of your windows operating system.

```
Command Prompt
   Link-local IPv6 Address . . . . . : fe80::b428:849d:99f2:8478%22
   IPv4 Address. . . . . . . . . . . : 192.168.56.1
   Subnet Mask . . . . . . . . . . . : 255.255.255.0
   Default Gateway . . . . . . . . . :

Wireless LAN adapter Local Area Connection* 2:

   Media State . . . . . . . . . . . : Media disconnected
   Connection-specific DNS Suffix  . :

Wireless LAN adapter Wi-Fi:

   Connection-specific DNS Suffix  . :
   IPv6 Address. . . . . . . . . . . : fd07:3ae:edc:0:b997:d00a:7d2f:897e
   Temporary IPv6 Address. . . . . . : fd07:3ae:edc:0:c4de:702d:645f:43a8
   Link-local IPv6 Address . . . . . : fe80::b997:d00a:7d2f:897e%5
   IPv4 Address. . . . . . . . . . . : 192.168.0.166
   Subnet Mask . . . . . . . . . . . : 255.255.255.0
   Default Gateway . . . . . . . . . : 192.168.0.1

Ethernet adapter Bluetooth Network Connection:

   Media State . . . . . . . . . . . : Media disconnected
   Connection-specific DNS Suffix  . :

Tunnel adapter isatap.{F77EAEC7-0145-448F-90CE-E580D1732ED1}:

   Media State . . . . . . . . . . . : Media disconnected
   Connection-specific DNS Suffix  . :

Tunnel adapter Teredo Tunneling Pseudo-Interface:

   Connection-specific DNS Suffix  . :
   IPv6 Address. . . . . . . . . . . : 2001:0:9d38:6abd:2433:a7b5:8c8f:93fb
   Link-local IPv6 Address . . . . . : fe80::2433:a7b5:8c8f:93fb%19
   Default Gateway . . . . . . . . . :

Tunnel adapter isatap.{AFA0432D-D4BA-480C-82FC-66C947E0885E}:

   Media State . . . . . . . . . . . : Media disconnected
   Connection-specific DNS Suffix  . :
```

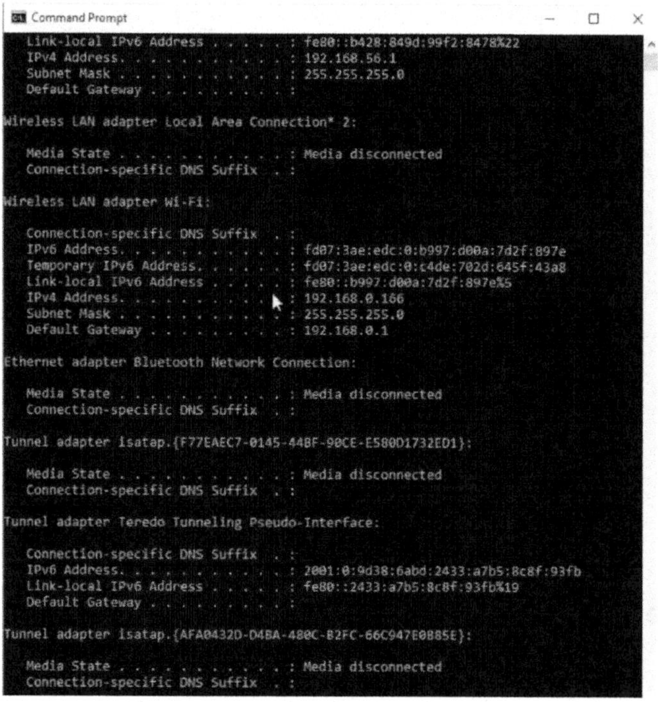

If you are connected through Wi-Fi, then you should look the details under Wireless Lan adapter Wi-Fi. If you are connected through Ethernet cable, then you need to look through Ethernet adapter.

What details we need to look at under the Wi-fi adapter or Ethernet adapter for assigning an IP address?

Let us first understand about IP address. Basically there are two types of IP addresses:

Static and Dynamic

When you assign a static IP address, the IP address remains same whenever you try to connect to the virtual machine irrespective of how many times you restart the machine.

You just need one single IP address to connect to a virtual machine in this case.

But in case of a dynamic IP address, it changes every time you start/stop or bounce (bring down and again bring it up again) the virtual machine. So, whenever you connect to your virtual machine, you need to login to the machine and get the IP address which is dynamically assigned to the machine and then you can try to connect it through your outside tools.

So eventually, we will try to have one static IP address for our virtual machine so that we do not have to go and check the IP addresses again and again.

Now we will check the IP address in the command prompt under Wireless Lan adapter Wi-Fi.

IPv4 Address - 192.168.0.166, in the above case, is the IP address of our Windows machine which is our home network.

The first 3 parts (192.168.0) of the IP addresses will be same for all the machines which are connected to the home network. The IP address for this virtual machine would be : 192.168.0.__

In the last part of the IP address, you can give anything between 1 and 255 and the number should be different than the home network IP address (in this case 166) as the two machines cannot have the same IP address. The recommended number is above 200 and below 255 always.

Suppose you have mobile phones, tablets and other PCs which are joined to your home network. Your router will assign the numbers starting from 1, 2, 3 and so on to these systems dynamically. So it is always better that you assign a very big number which would never clash with the other systems IP addresses.

Next is Gateway IP. You can see in the above screenshot that the Default Gateway IP is given in the last line under Wireless LAN adapter Wi-Fi (192.168.0.1).

The GATEWAY IP will remain same for all your virtual machines as this IP is nothing but your router IP through which the machine communicate to the internet.

If we do not give this Gateway IP in our virtual machine IP details, then we will not be able to use the internet on our virtual machine.

Then we have NETMASK IP which you can see as Subnet mask IP under Wireless Lan adapter Wi-Fi (in this case 255.255.255.0).

Also when you work with Linux, you need to enter one Primary DNS IP address. It is actually the same as your Gateway IP (192.168.0.1).

Primary DNS = Gateway IP = 192.168.0.1

So we have our Virtual Machine IP Details ready:

IP ADDRESS: 192.168.0.200
GATEWAY IP: 192.168.0.1
NETMASK IP: 255.255.255.0

PRIMARY DNS: 192.168.0.1

The above details are required when we install Linux on our blank virtual machine.

We need to make a couple of changes in the settings of the virtual machine so that it can communicate to the internet.

Right click on the virtual machine and go to the Settings option

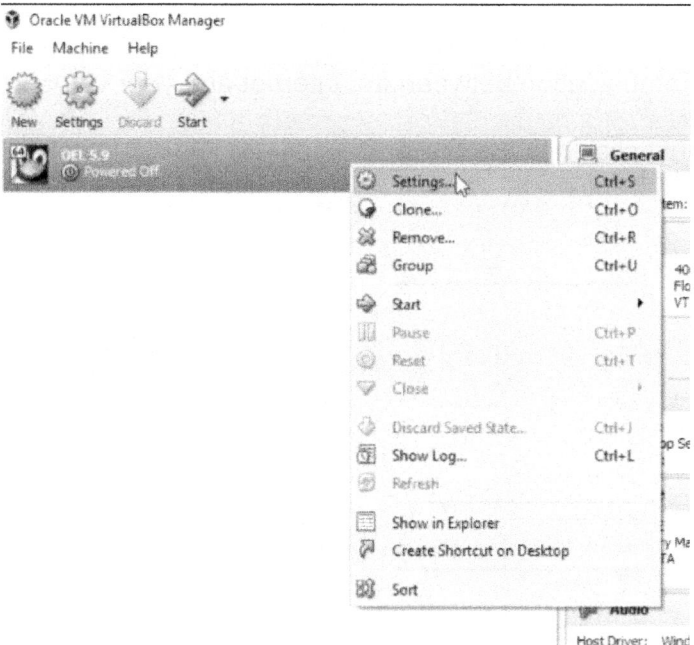

In the settings tab, come down and click Network

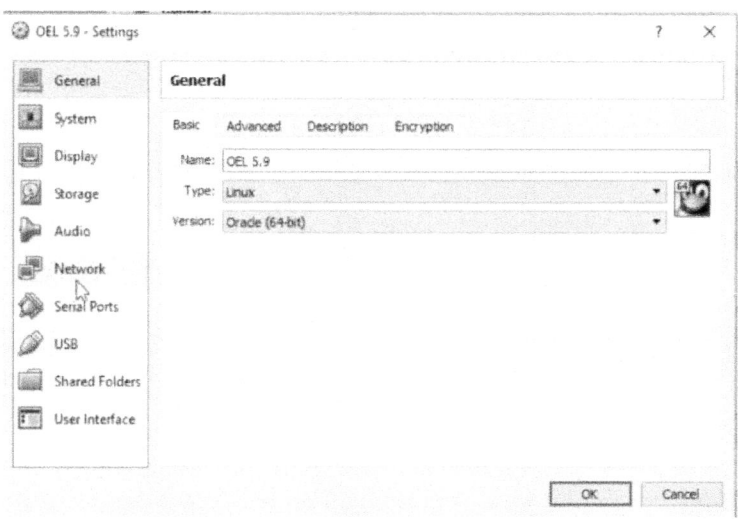

Now in the Network screen, make sure that one adapter is attached (tick mark should be there in the box beside Enable Network Adapter).

In the drop down "Attached to", select **Bridged Adapter** for enabling the communication between the internet and your virtual machine.

Then just click on OK button.

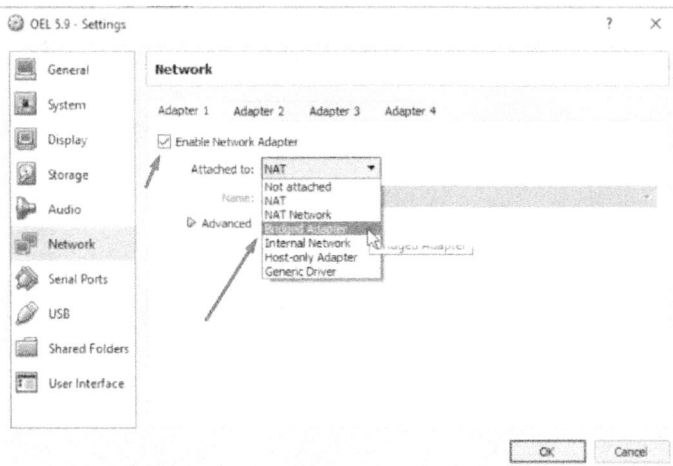

## CHAPTER 3

Install Oracle Linux on VirtualBox

How to download OEL?

In this lesson, we will learn how to download the OEL (Oracle Enterprise Linux).

Go to **edelivery.oracle.com**

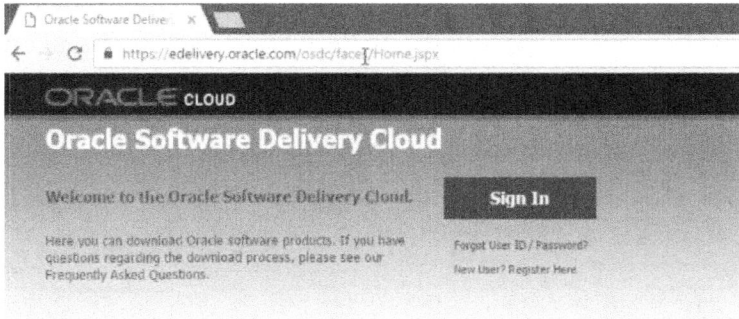

This is the cloud based website provided by Oracle to deliver all the softwares that is developed by Oracle. For some of the software, you need the license but most of the software are available here for a direct download and are ready to use.

If you have an account, directly Sign in or else you need to register as a new user.

Once you sign in, type Oracle Linux in the search box.

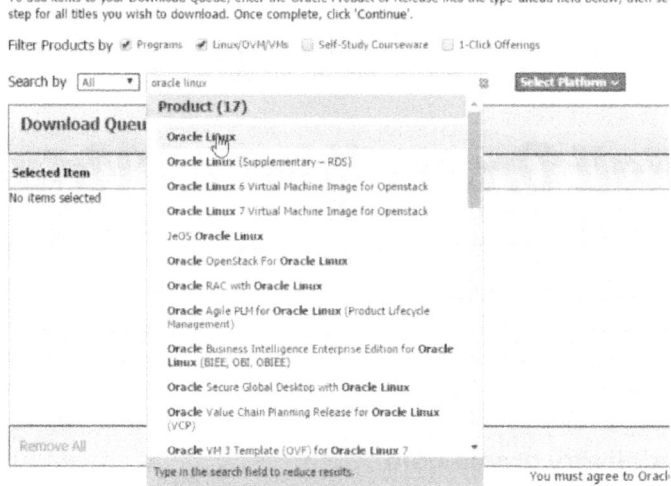

And then choose the platform as 64-bit and click on Select button

Now that the product Oracle Linux has been selected, click on Continue

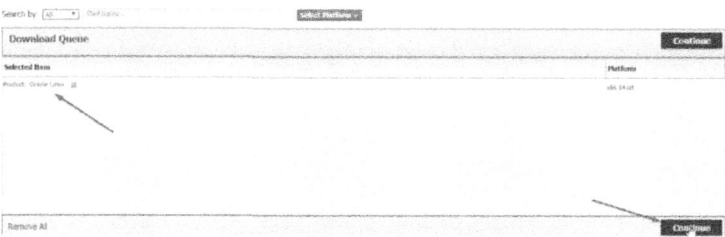

By default, the latest released version will be selected. As of today the latest release is Oracle Linux 7.2. But we will select 5.9 version as we will install Linux 5.9 for our course by going into Select Alternate release.

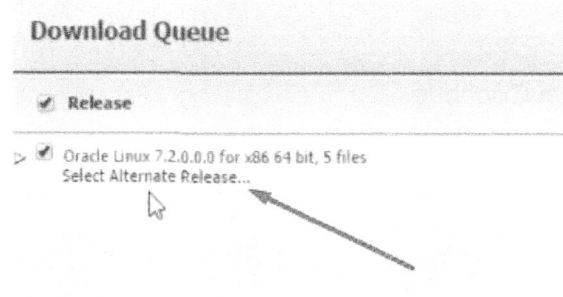

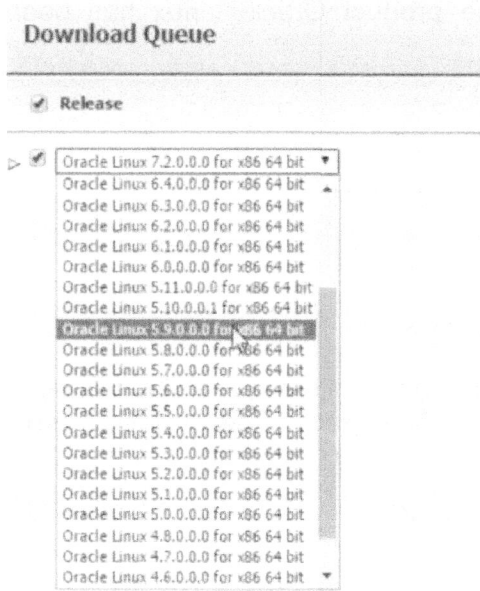

Then click on Continue.

Accept the terms and conditions and click on Continue again

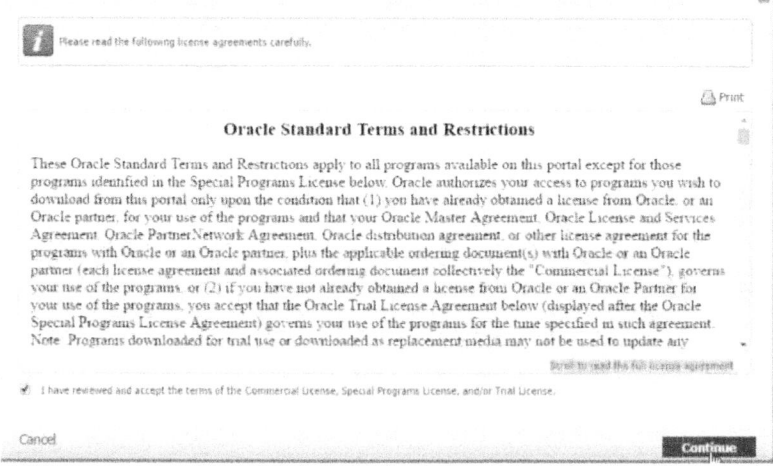

You will now get the list of the files that you need to download. You will choose the file with the largest size which is your OEL file.

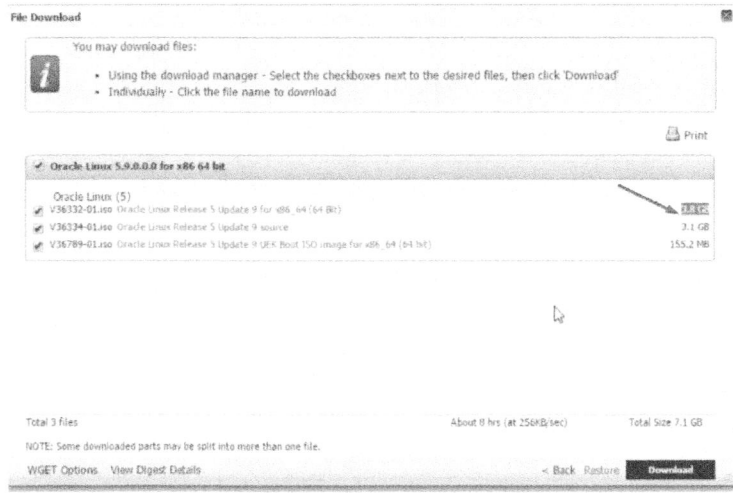

Click on the link and the download will start.

Remember that the file names will be different than the original file names once downloaded. So you need to rename the file once downloaded so that it makes more sense on your local file system. So here we will rename it from v36332-01.iso to OEL 5.9 which is relevant for us.

Installing OEL 5.9 on VirtualBox

Let us start the installation of OEL 5.9 on our blank virtual machine.

First, we need to insert the .iso file into the cd drive of OEL 5.9 blank virtual machine.

Once try to start the virtual machine OEL 5.9 by clicking on Start. There is nothing in the virtual machine that it can boot up from. There is no .iso file, no hard disk, no operating system installed on to it. So close or power off the virtual machine. Now we will tell the virtual machine that we are going to install the OEL 5.9.

Go to Settings by right clicking on the virtual machine:

Now come to Storage option and you will see that your cd drive is Empty.

You need to browse into your cd drive. In my case, the .iso file is getting listed as I have used the OEL 5.9.iso file once. In your case, you will not see the list and you need to click on **Choose Virtual Optical Disk File** and locate your .iso file onto your Windows machine.

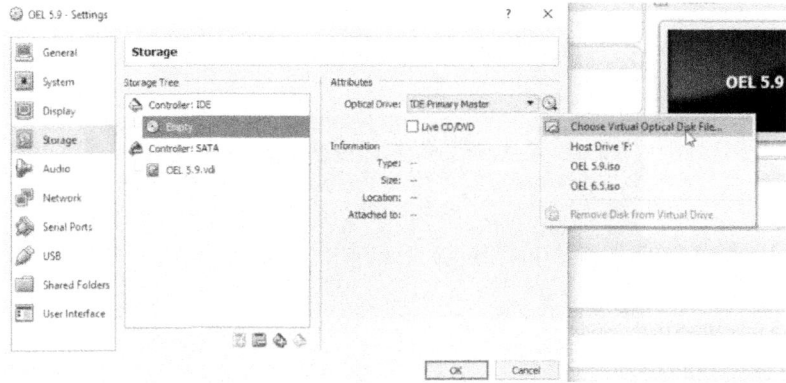

Now the .ISO file is loaded in the cd drive of the virtual machine. So click on Ok button.

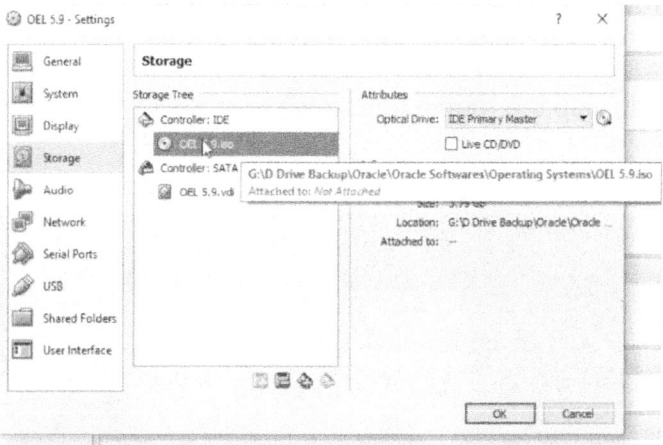

Now start your virtual machine using Start button from the top Menu.

This will start the virtual machine using the .iso file and the .iso file will help us to install OEL 5.9 on the machine.

Now click inside the virtual machine and hit Enter.

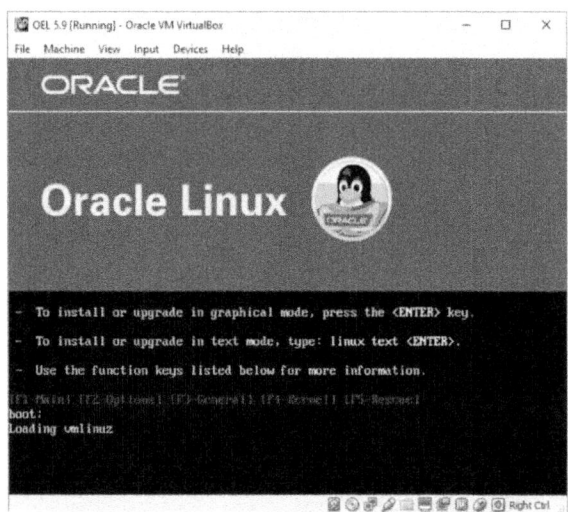

Once you click inside the virtual machine, the mouse pointer will go off. To come out of the virtual machine, you need to press right Ctrl key.

But we will be staying inside the virtual machine. There will be couple of options that we need to come across.

First of all, skip the media test.

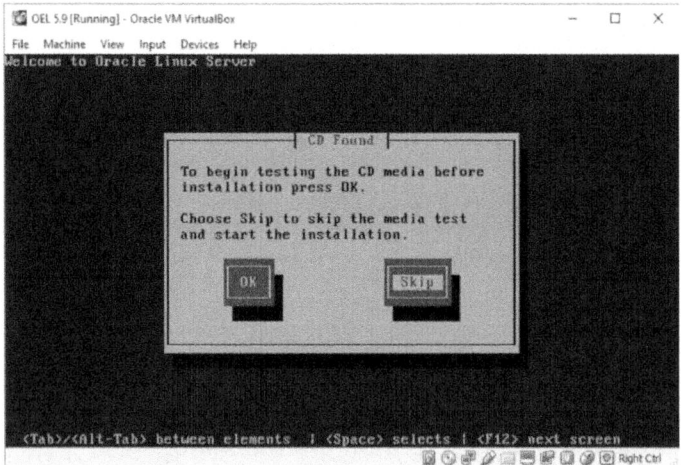

Then hit Enter. You will get the OEL installation screen.

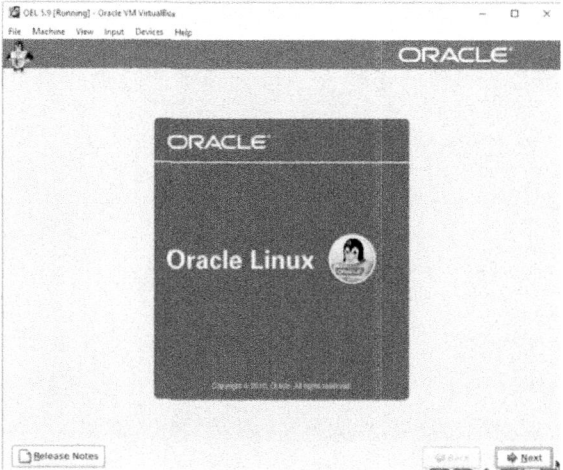

Click on Next. Choose the default language option which is English.

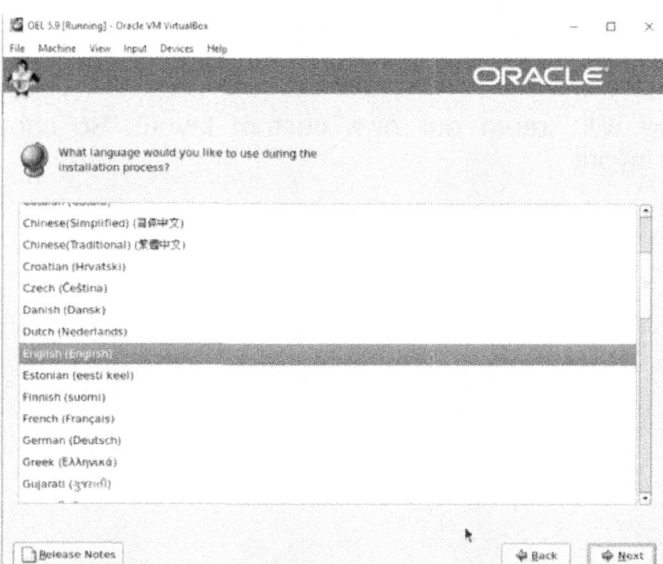

Click on the Next button. Choose the default keyboard U.S.English

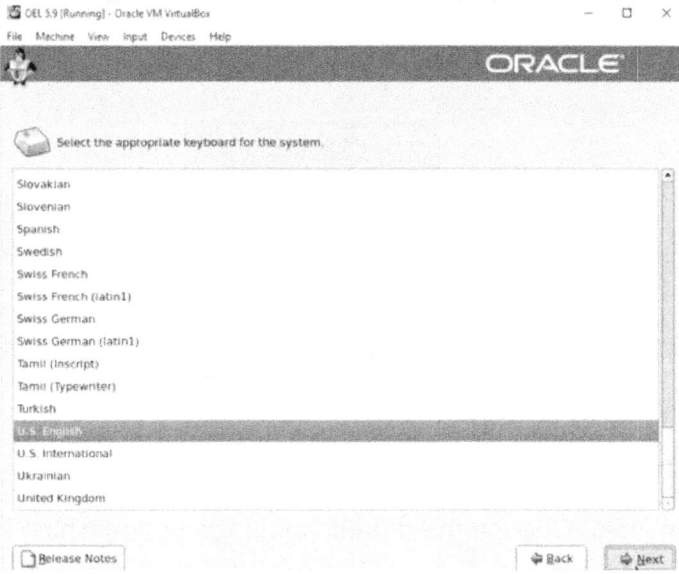

Click on Next

Now we will create our own custom layout. So choose Create custom layout.

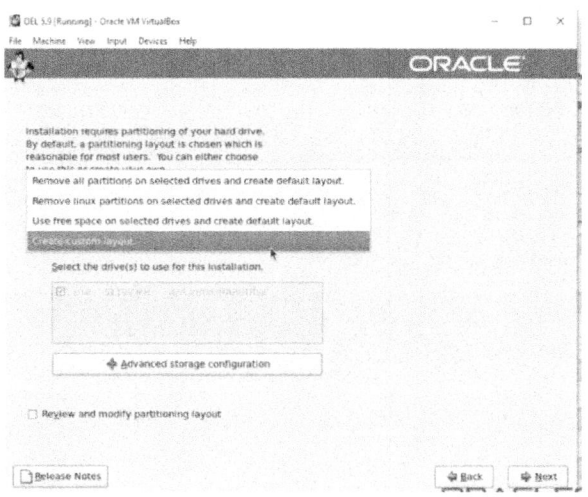

Click on Next

We will see the entire 50GB hard disk in the screen now.

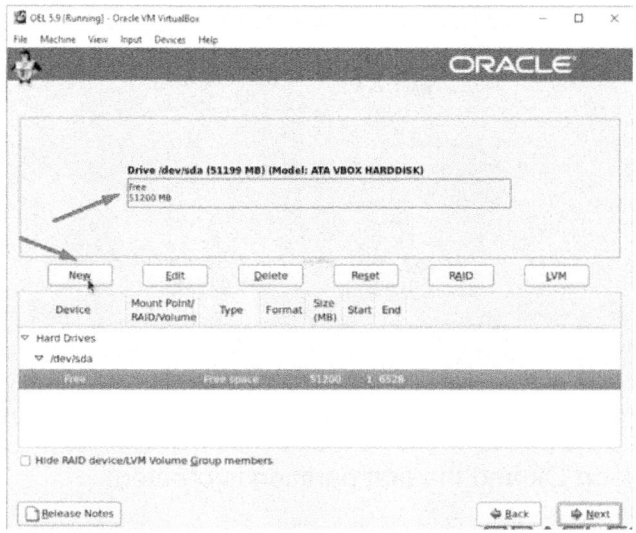

Click on New to create our first partition.

The first partition would be "/" (root mount point). We will allocate 10GB to this mount point.

Note: In windows, Mount point is called as drive.

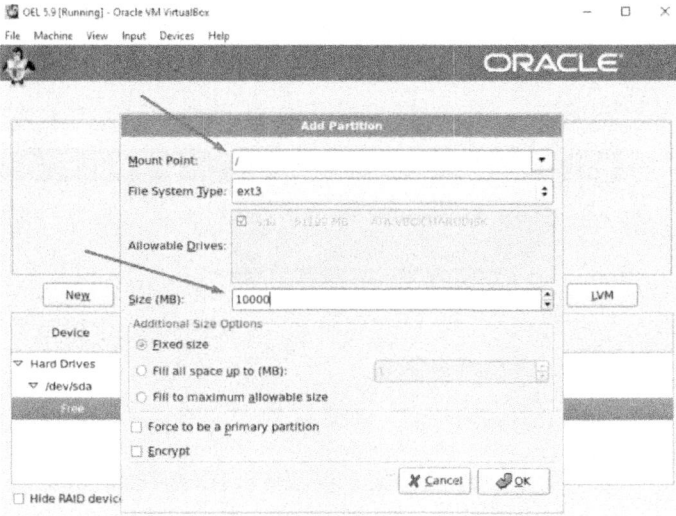

Now click on Ok and the first partition is created.

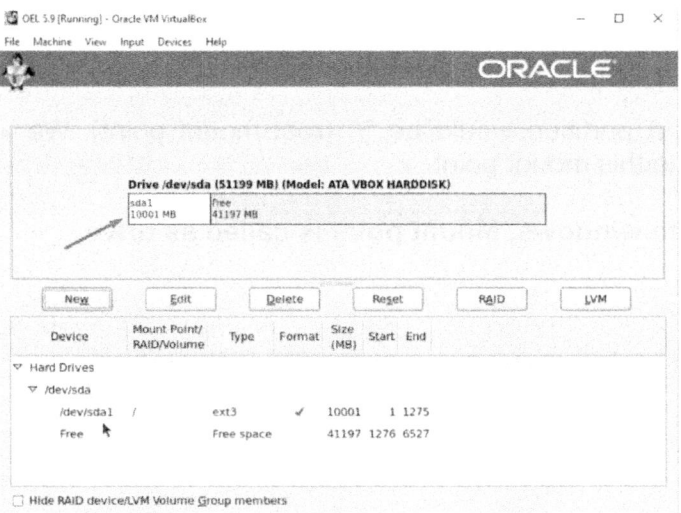

Now create another partition as "/boot" mount point and allocate 512 MB to the boot mount point.

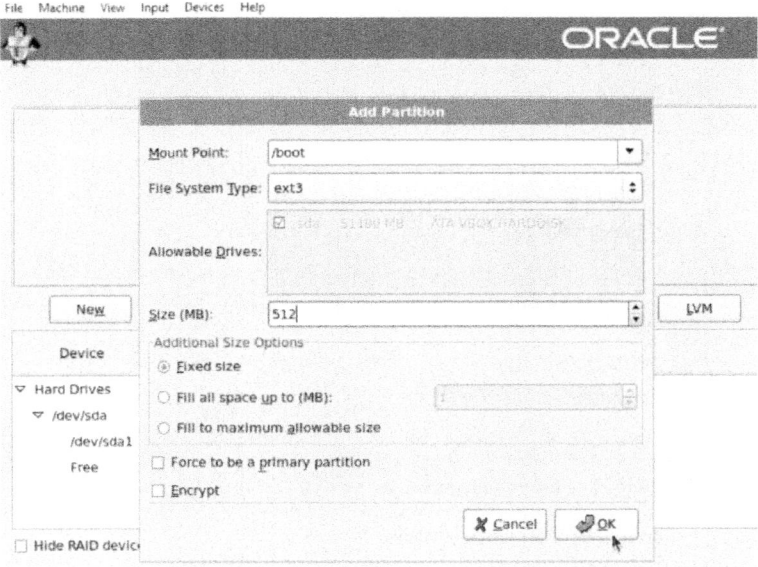

Click on Ok

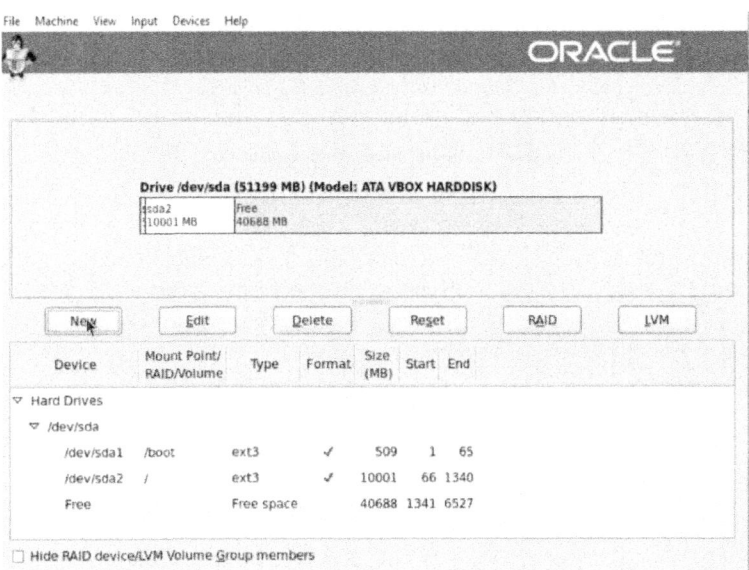

Now we will create the Swap file system. Generally Swap should be double the size of RAM. So we would allocate 8GB (as in our case, we have 4GB RAM).

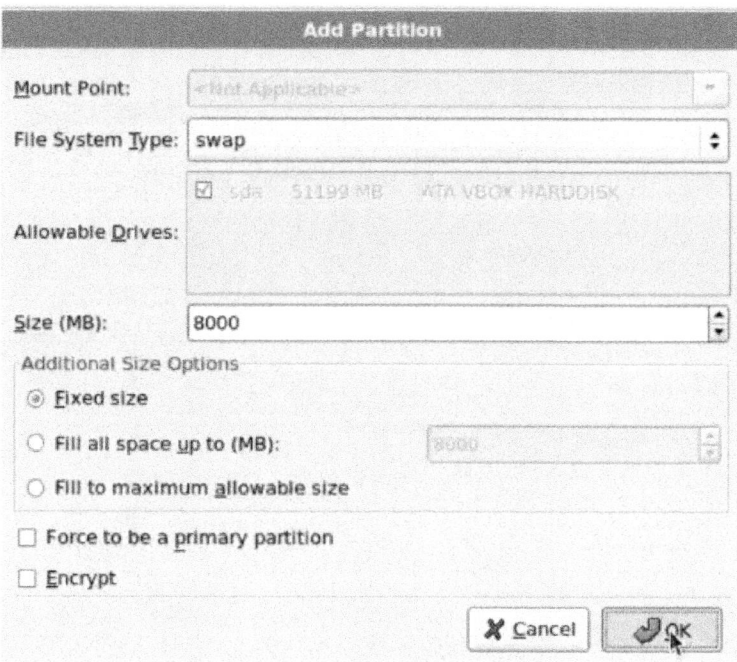

Click on OK and the screen will look like this:

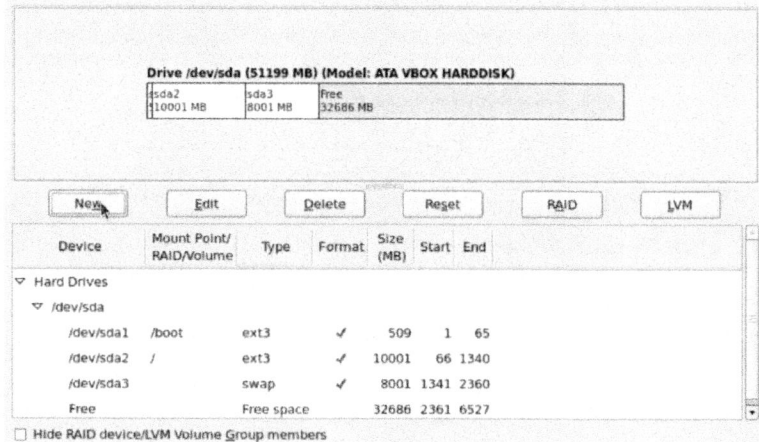

Now from the 32GB left, let us create first User mount point as /u01 and assign 10 GB to it.

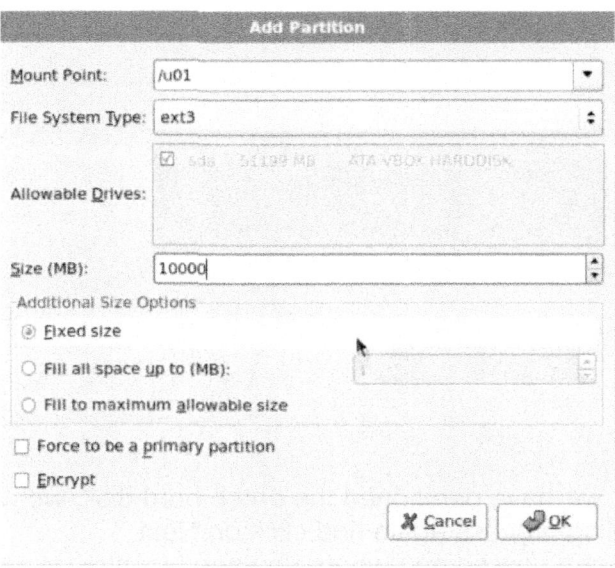

We will create another user mount point /u02 and choose the option as fill to maximum allowable size.

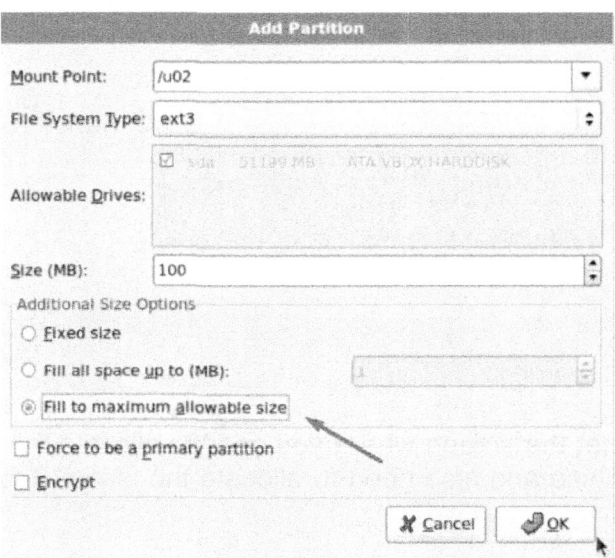

The entire 22 GB is allocated to the /u02 mount point.

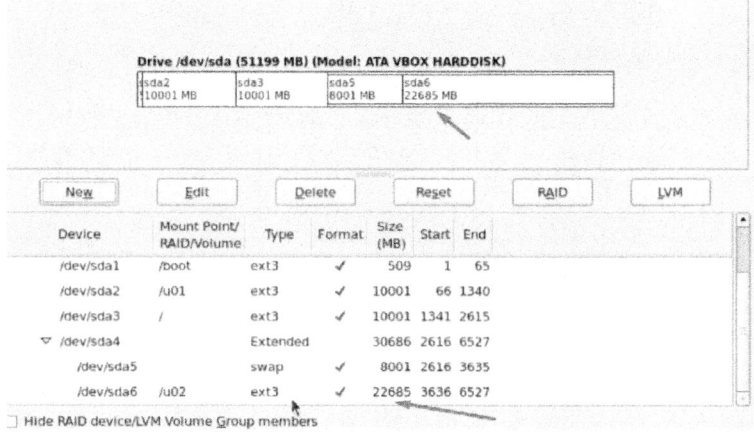

Now that we have partitioned the entire hard disk, we will proceed to the installing process again and click on Next
You will get a new screen where you need to click on Next.

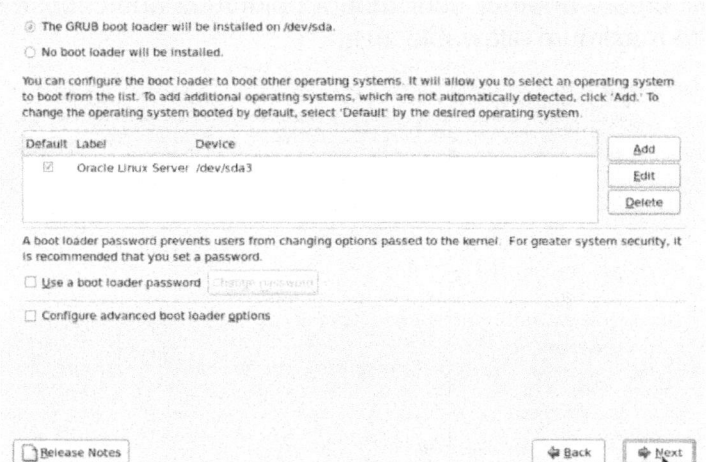

You will get the screen where you need to allocate the host name to your machine and also need to allocate the static IP for your virtual machine.

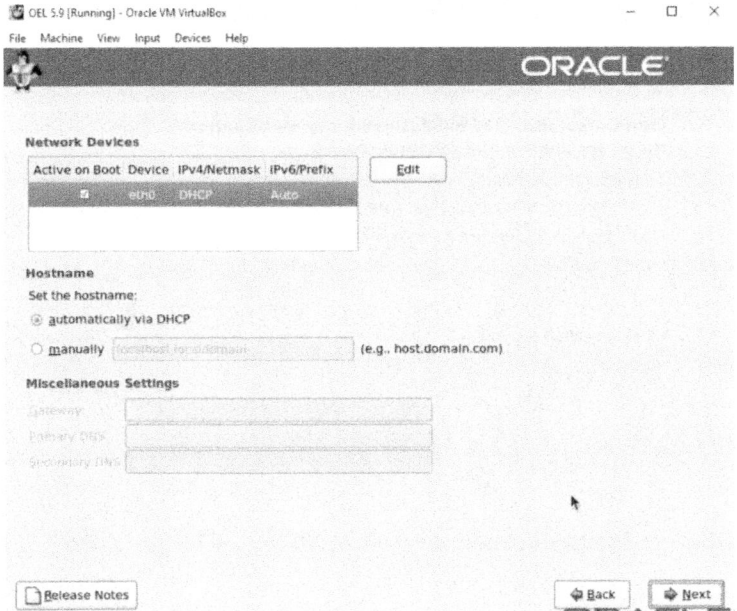

Choose the Ethernet adapter eth0 and click on Edit button

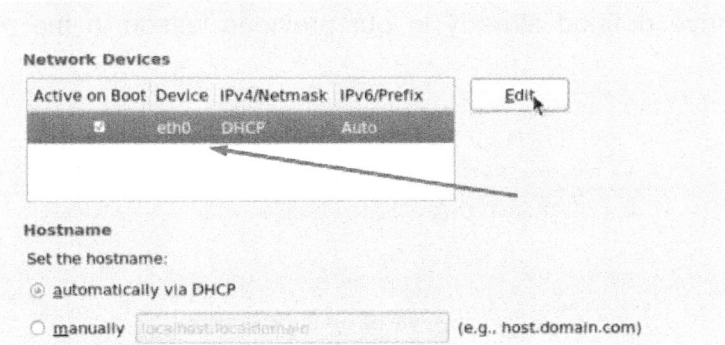

On the next screen:

- You need to disable the IPv6 support (remove the tick mark from the box beside Enable IPv6 support) as we are not using it.
- Under IPv4 support, choose Manual configuration option.
- Under the IP address, give the IP address that we have defined in the previous lesson for our virtual machine.
- Under the Prefix (Netmask), put the Netmask IP that we

have defined in the previous lesson.

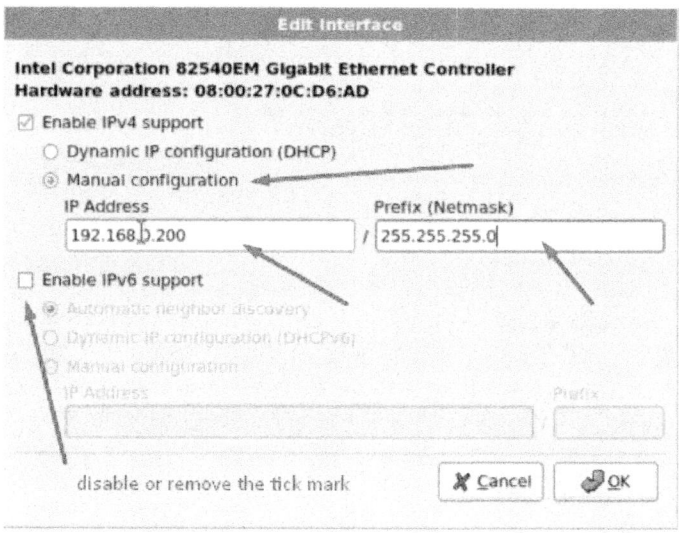

Now click on OK button.

Now you need to assign the Gateway IP and the Primary DNS which we have defined already in our previous lesson in the respective fields.

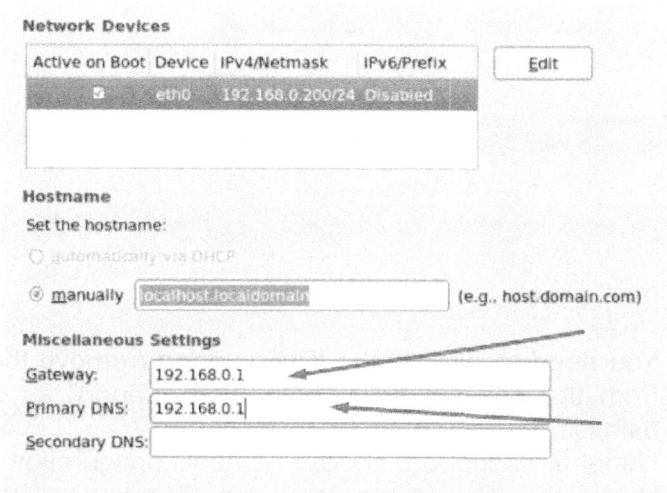

Now you also have to assign a host name to your virtual machine.

This host name will help you to identify the virtual machine in a human readable format. Rather than remembering all the IP addresses, you can remember the name of the virtual machine.

We will give oel5.oraclegenesis.com as the host name for this virtual machine.

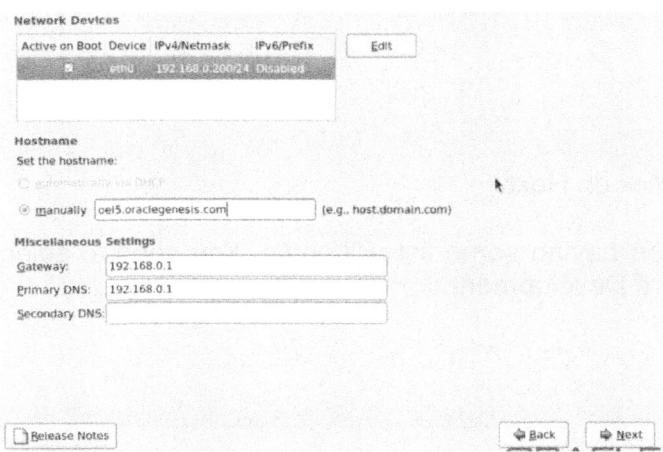

Now click on Next and you will get a screen where you need to choose the time zone.

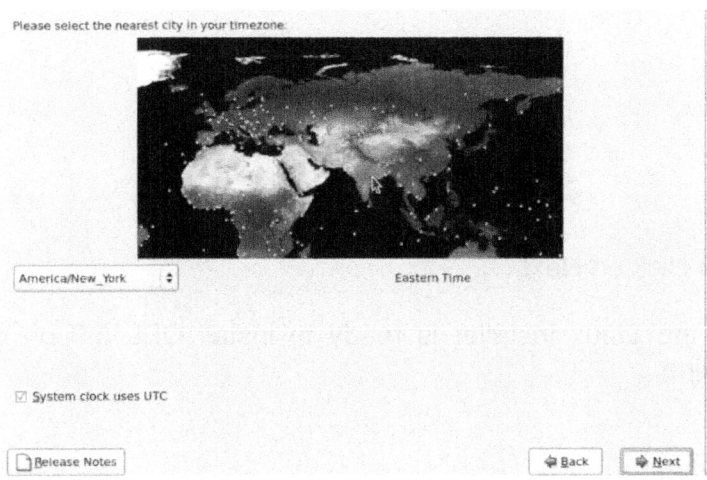

Click on Next

Now give a Password for admin and confirm it.

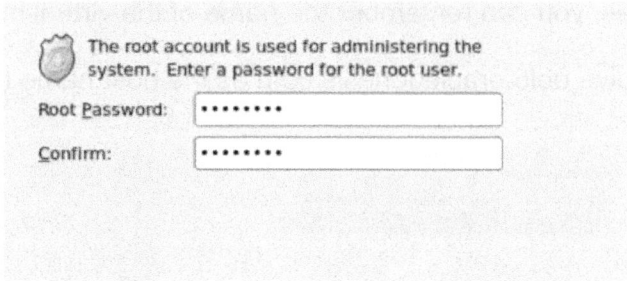

Then click on Next

A screen having some list will come. You need to select the option Software Development.

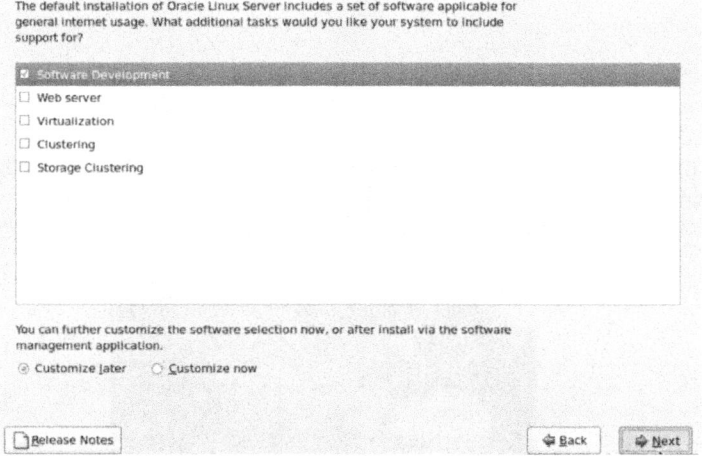

Again click on Next.

Now the Linux installer is ready to install OEL 5.9 on our virtual machine.

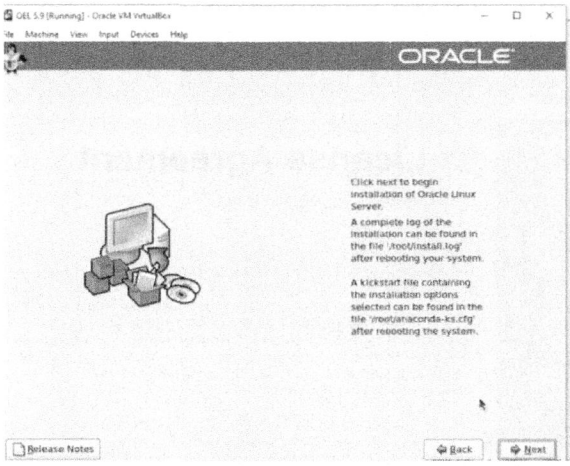

Click on Next to begin the installation. The installation will start.

OEL 5.9 Post Installation Steps

Once the installation of OEL 5.9 is done, your system will reboot. After the reboot, there are some steps that you need to complete. These steps will remain same for any number of installations that you do at least for the eBooks or courses that we have on dbagenesis.

Now click inside the virtual machine and click on Forward.

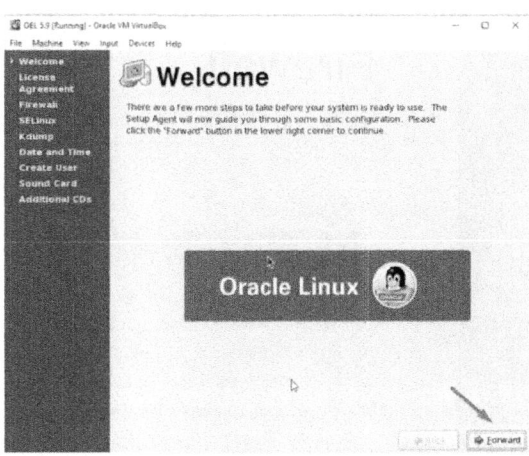

Accept the License agreement

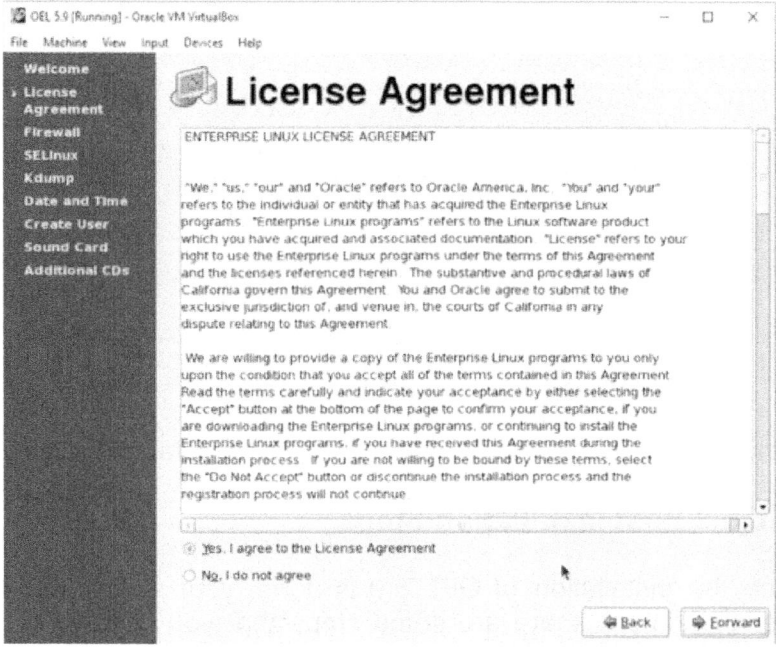

Disable the Firewall as we want the virtual machines to be connected to other virtual machines.

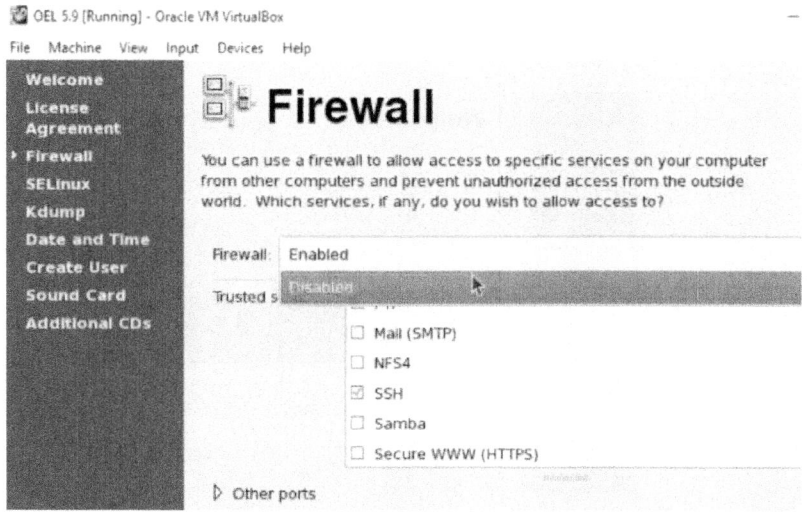

It will prompt you for a warning. Click Yes

Then you need to disable the SELinux

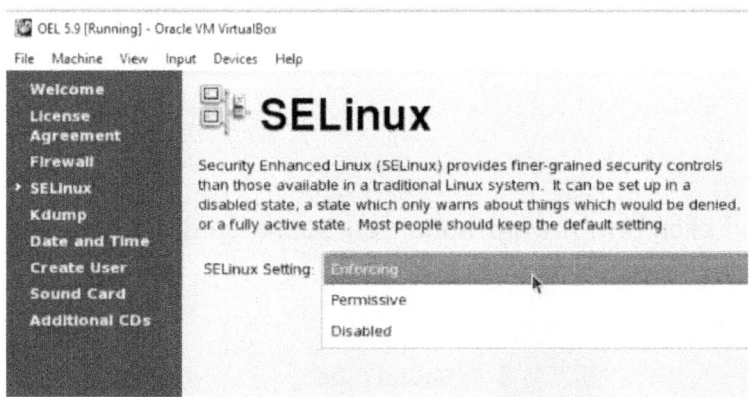

Then click Forward and accept the default date and time and click Forward again.

Then you will come to a screen which will prompt to create a user. At this stage, we are not going to create any user.
So click Forward again

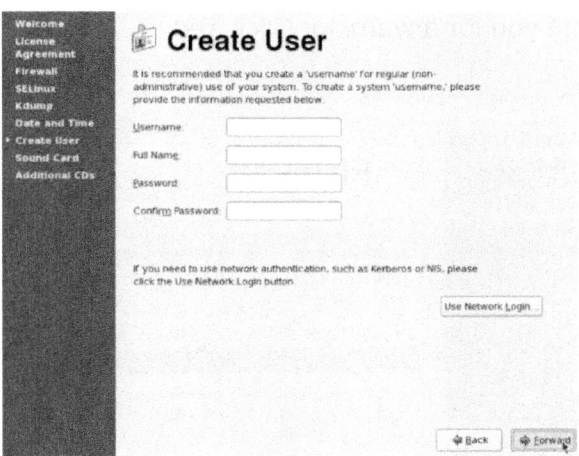

It will ask you to Continue or create account. You will choose Continue.

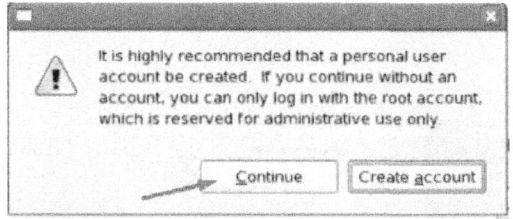

Again click on Forward button on Sound card screen as we do not have to do anything on this screen.

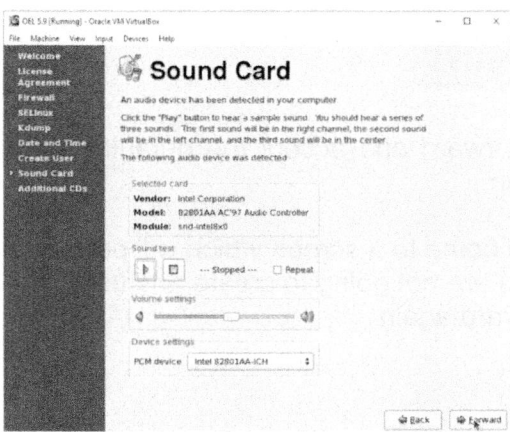

Click on Finish button to finish your post installation steps.

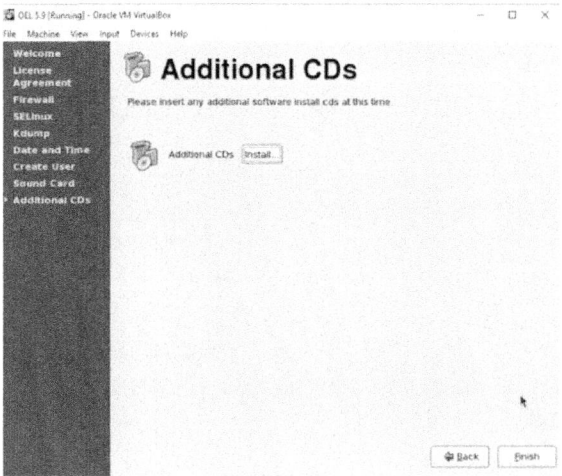

Once you click on Finish, the machine will reboot and finally your OEL 5.9 installation is done.

Installing OEL 6.5 on VirtualBox

In the previous lesson, we learnt about the installation of OEL 5.9. It is the old version and I would recommend installing the new version which is OEL 6.5.

In this lesson, we will learn how to install OEL 6.5 on the virtual machine.

Click on New. A window will open where you need to give a name to your virtual machine and select the type and version of it.
Here we will give the name as OEL 6.5 and select the type as Linux and version as Oracle 64-bit.

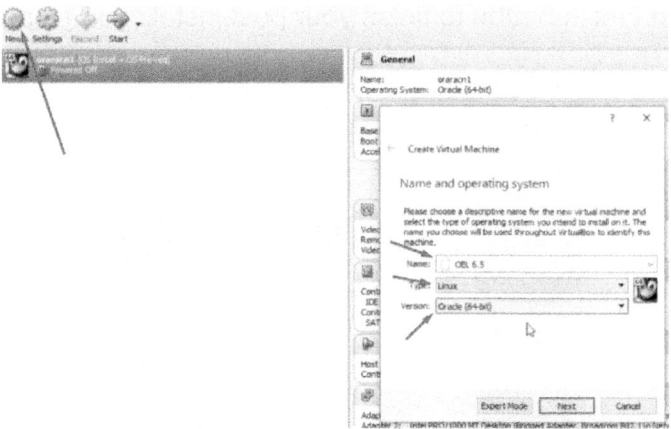

Click on Next

Then we need to allocate 4GB RAM to the virtual machine.

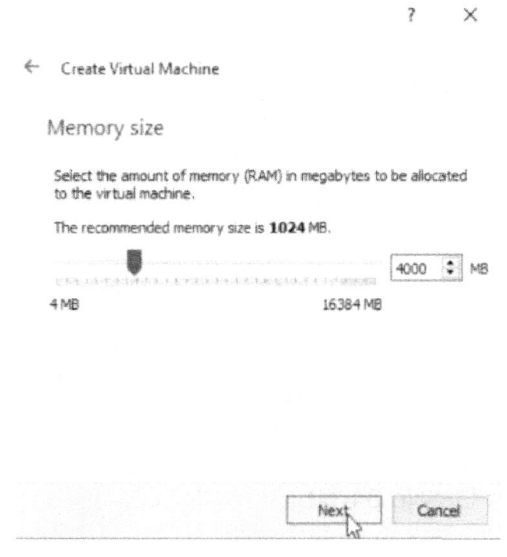

Now choose the option to Create a virtual hard disk

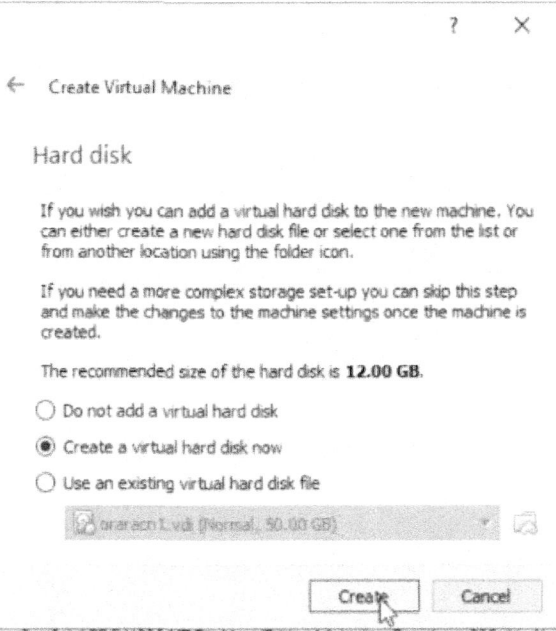

We will go with the default option VDI (Virtualbox disk image)

Click on Next

Then choose the option "Dynamically allocated"

Then we will give the hard disk size of our virtual machine as 50 GB

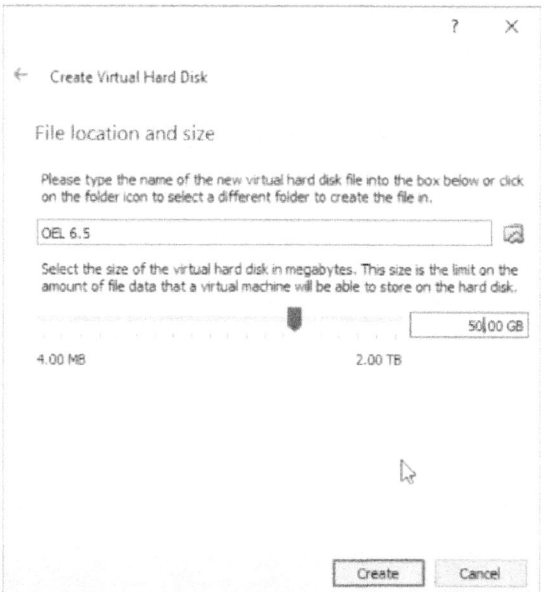

Then click on Create.

On the left hand side of the screen, we can see the OEL 6.5 virtual machine has been created.

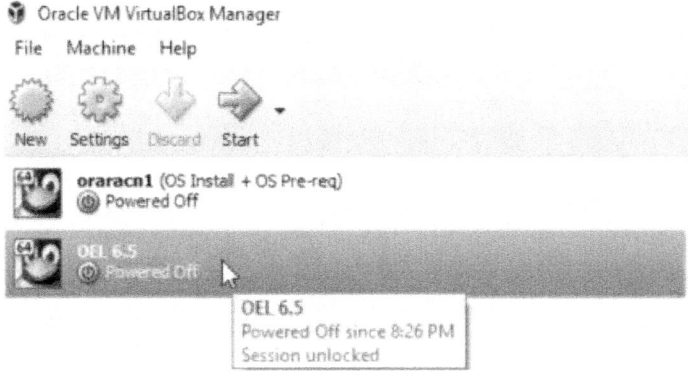

Now we need to install OEL 6.5 on to the virtual machine. For this, we need to insert the .iso file inside the cd drive of the machine.

We will go to Settings of the virtual machine by right clicking on the virtual machine.

Then choose the Storage option under settings. You can see that the cd drive is Empty.

You need to browse and navigate to the .iso file in your system.

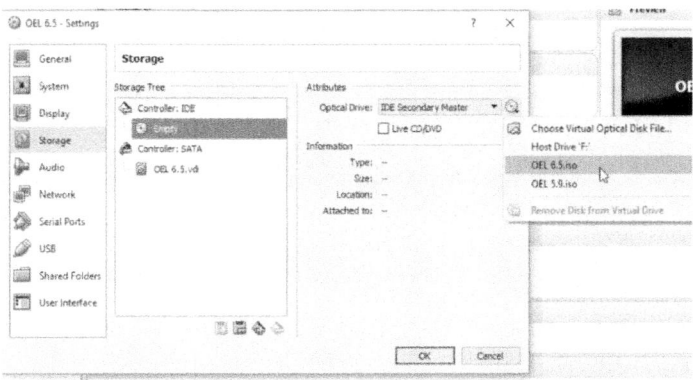

In the above screenshot, it is already in the list as I already have installed it. It will not be available for you like this. So you need to browse through your local folders and load it.

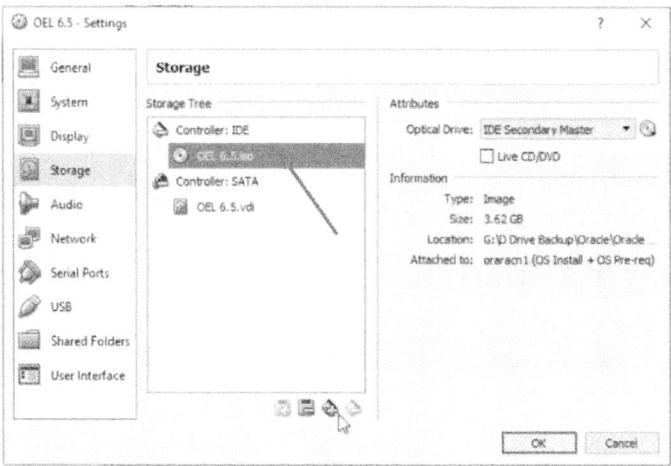

Now we will make sure that internet communication is enabled on this virtual machine.

- Go to Network in Settings
- See that the Network adapter is enabled (tick mark)
- Choose the option Bridged Adapter in the drop down under Attached to.

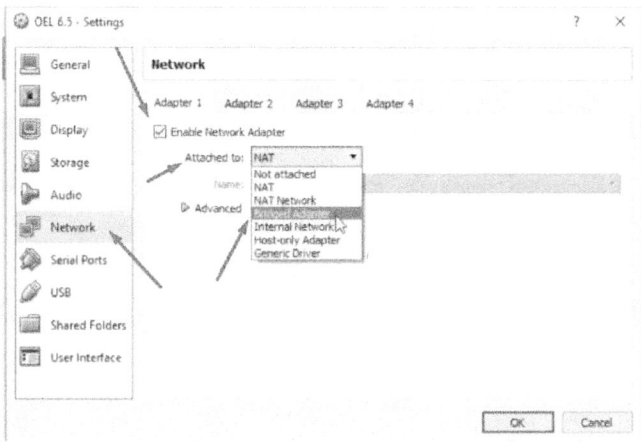

Then we will go to System option under Settings

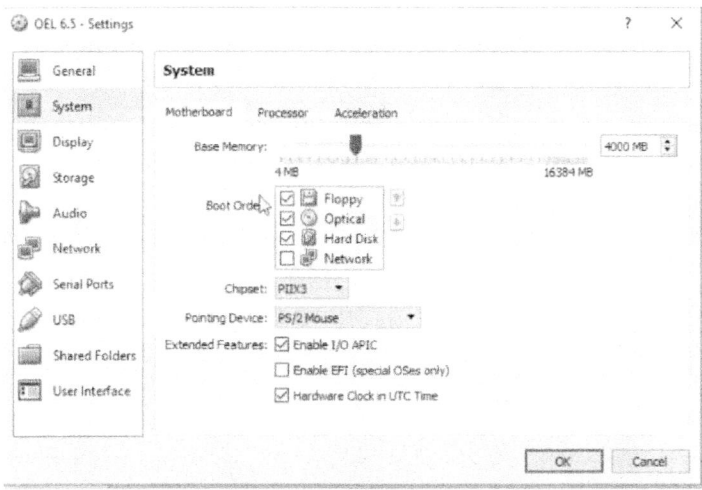

Disable the Floppy drive under Boot order box and bring it down. Make sure that only Optical and Hard disk options are tick marked.

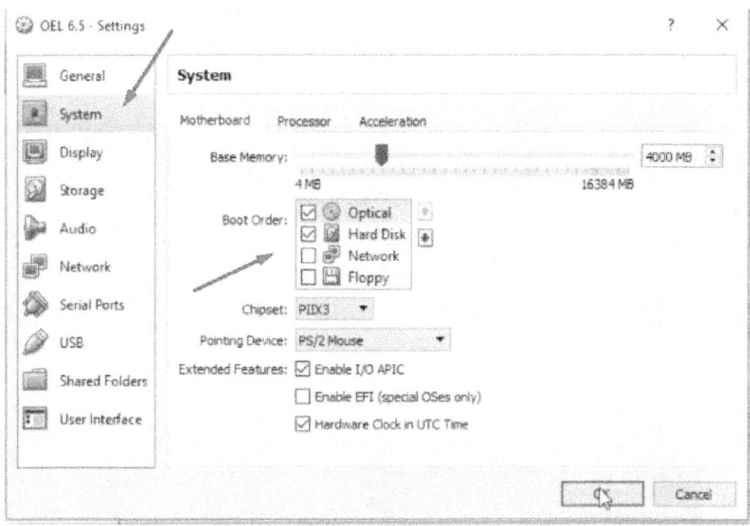

Click on Ok button.

Now we are ready to install OEL 6.5 on our virtual machine. Select the virtual machine and click on Start.

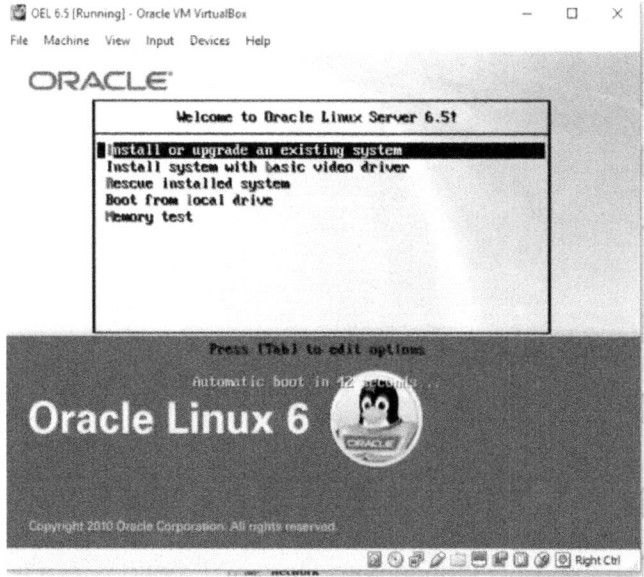

Now click inside the virtual machine and hit Enter

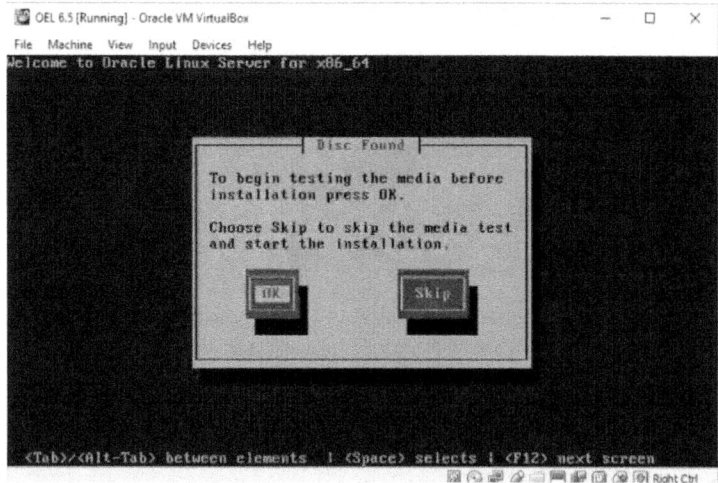

Now skip the media test

Then the Linux installer will start

Click on Next

Select the default language as English

Then select the Keyboard language as U.S.English

From here, the screens and options will be different from the installation in OEL 5.9.

Now select the option Basic Storage Devices

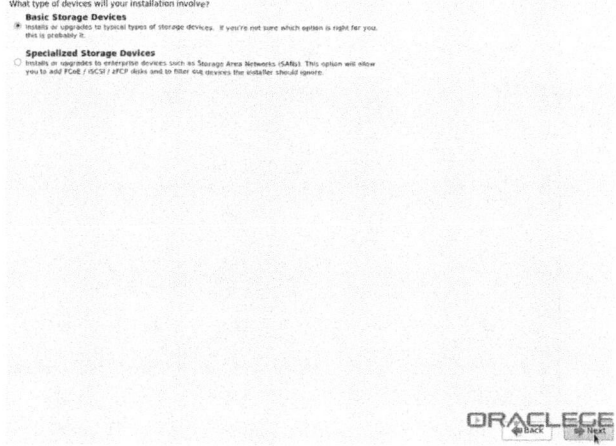

Now it will ask to remove all the data from the 50 GB hard disk that is allocated to the virtual machine.
So we will click on Yes, discard any data

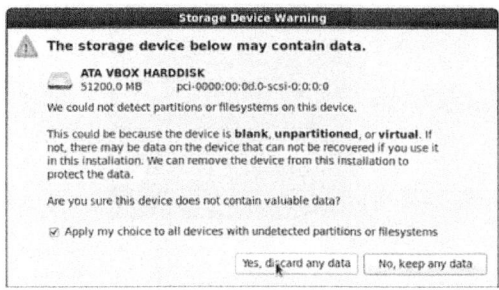

Now we need to give a host name to the machine. It is always good to give a name to the IP address which makes it easier to remember.

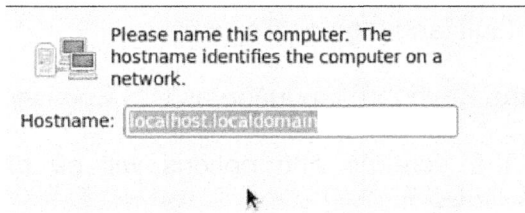

We will give the host name as oel6.oraclegenesis.com and click on configure network.

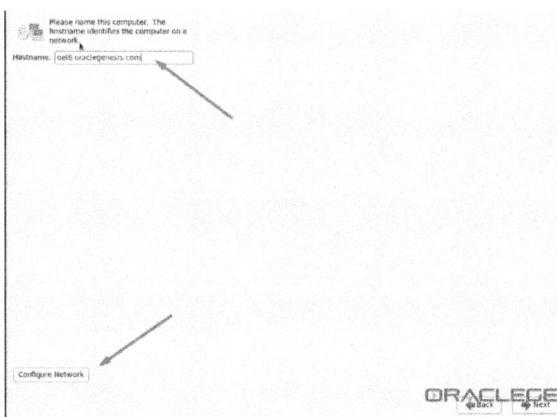

Now a window will open. You need to choose the ethernet card eth0 and click on Edit.

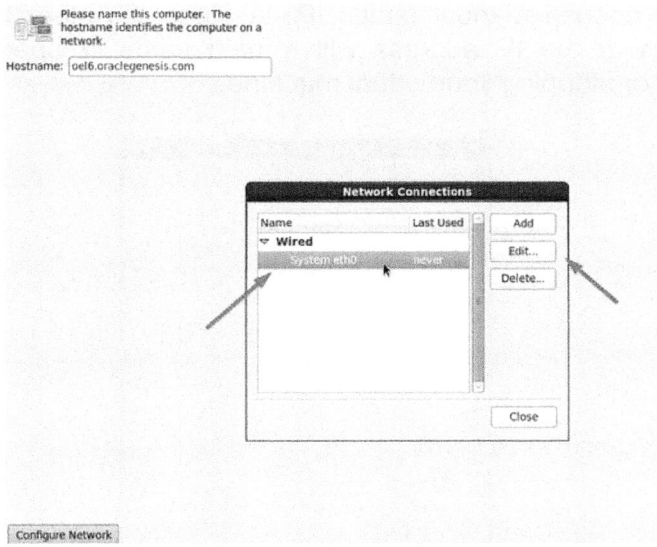

Then choose the option Connect automatically so that your network is always connected whenever you start your machine.

Then we need to choose IPv4 Settings. The default option in method field will be Automatic (DHCP) which is dynamic allocation.

We will choose Manual (static IP) in place of Automatic. This will ensure that the IP address will remain same irrespective of you starting or stopping your virtual machine.

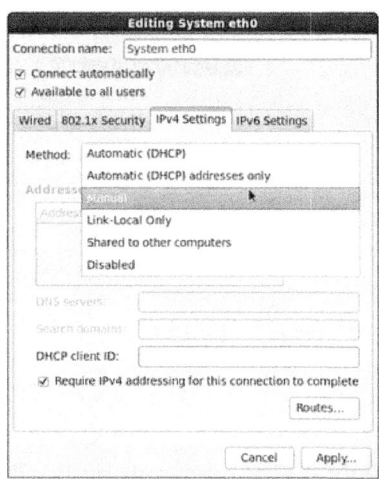

Now we will give the IP address in the respective fields.

So we have entered the IP address as 192.168.0.219
Netmask IP as 255.255.255.0

Gateway IP as 192.168.0.1
DNS server as 192.168.0.1

Then click on Apply

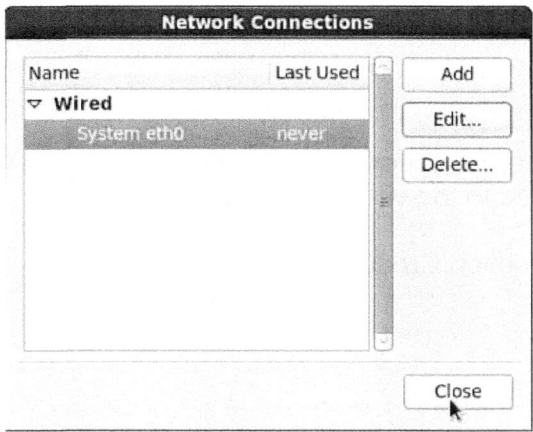

Close the above window.
Click on Next
It will ask to choose the time zone.
Choose your time zone and click on Next

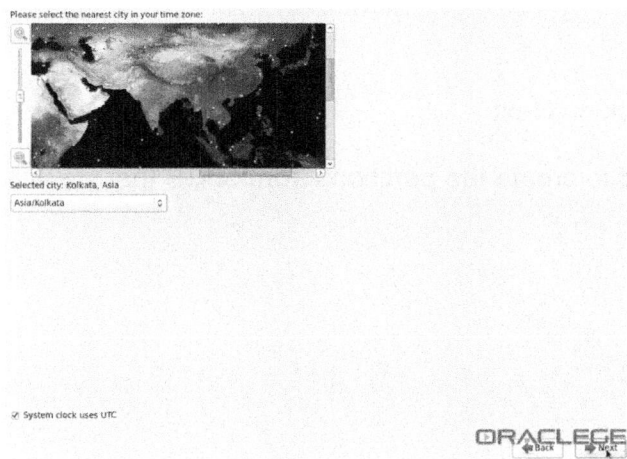

Now give a root password and confirm it by again typing it in the next field.

> The root account is used for administering the system. Enter a password for the root user.
>
> Root Password: ••••••••
>
> Confirm: ••••••••|

Now we have the option to create partitions to the hard disk that we have allocated to the virtual machine.

Choose the option Create custom layout

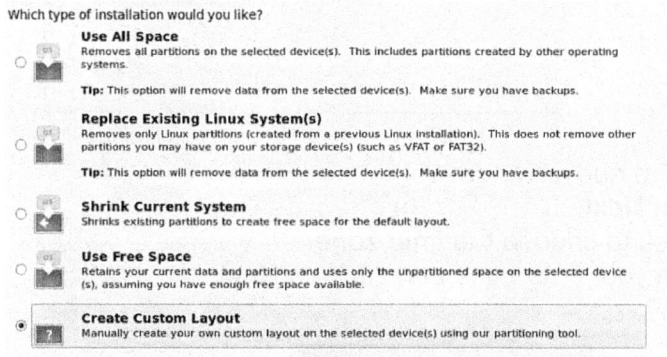

Which type of installation would you like?

Use All Space
Removes all partitions on the selected device(s). This includes partitions created by other operating systems.

Tip: This option will remove data from the selected device(s). Make sure you have backups.

Replace Existing Linux System(s)
Removes only Linux partitions (created from a previous Linux installation). This does not remove other partitions you may have on your storage device(s) (such as VFAT or FAT32).

Tip: This option will remove data from the selected device(s). Make sure you have backups.

Shrink Current System
Shrinks existing partitions to create free space for the default layout.

Use Free Space
Retains your current data and partitions and uses only the unpartitioned space on the selected device(s), assuming you have enough free space available.

Create Custom Layout
Manually create your own custom layout on the selected device(s) using our partitioning tool.

Then click on Next

We need to create the partitions from 50GB that we have allocated.

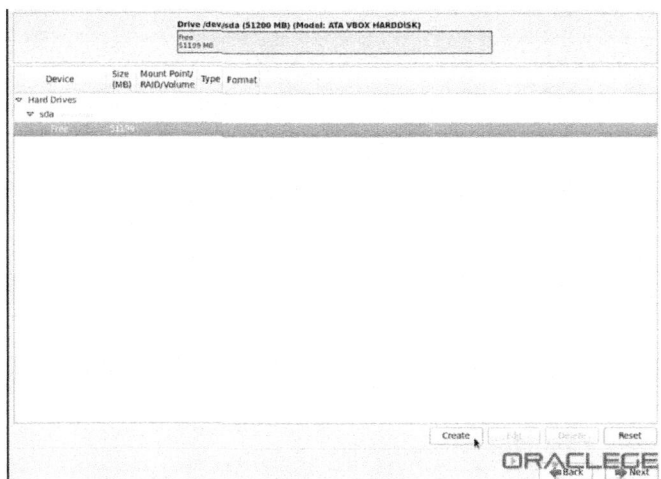

We will go with the option Standard Partition and click Create

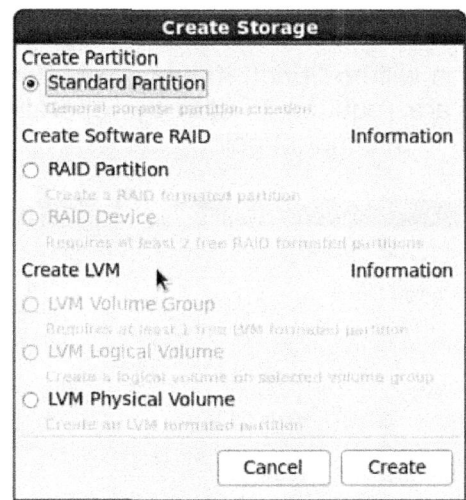

The first partition will be "/" (root) mount point and we will allocate 10 GB to it.

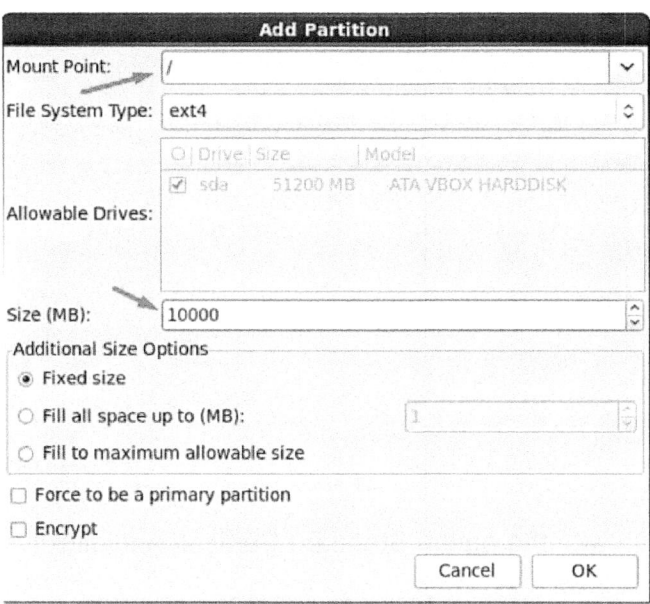

The next partition will be "/boot" mount point. This mount point holds the files which are required to start the operating system. We will allocate 512 MB to this mount point.

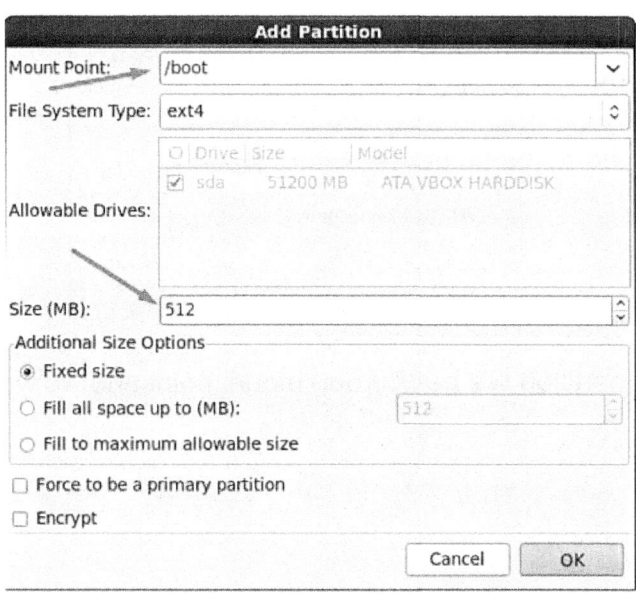

We will now create the Swap file system. Generally the size of the

Swap should be double the RAM size. But most of the times, RAM plus 2GB will work.

So we will give 6GB to the Swap file system.

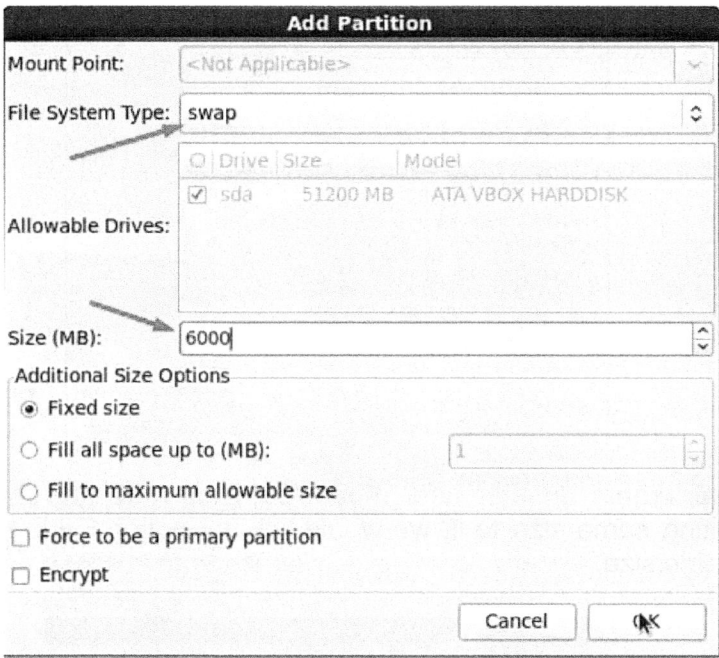

We have allocated the required mount points for our system to work well like / mount point, boot mount point and Swap.

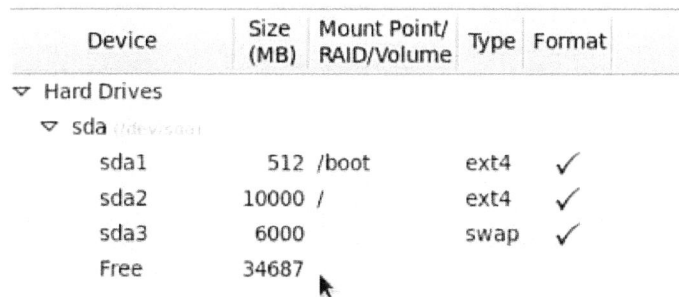

Device	Size (MB)	Mount Point/ RAID/Volume	Type	Format
▽ Hard Drives				
▽ sda				
sda1	512	/boot	ext4	✓
sda2	10000	/	ext4	✓
sda3	6000		swap	✓
Free	34687			

Now the left over space 34 GB can be used to create multiple user mount points. We will create the first user mount point as /u01 and allocate 10 GB to it.

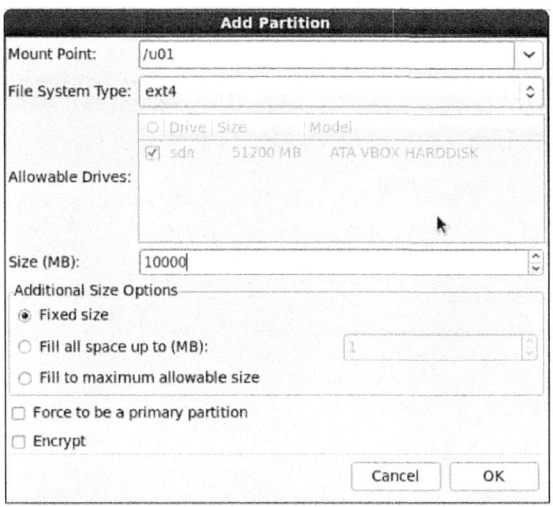

We will create another user mount point as /u02 and rather than allocating some size to it, we would tick the option Fill to maximum allowable size.

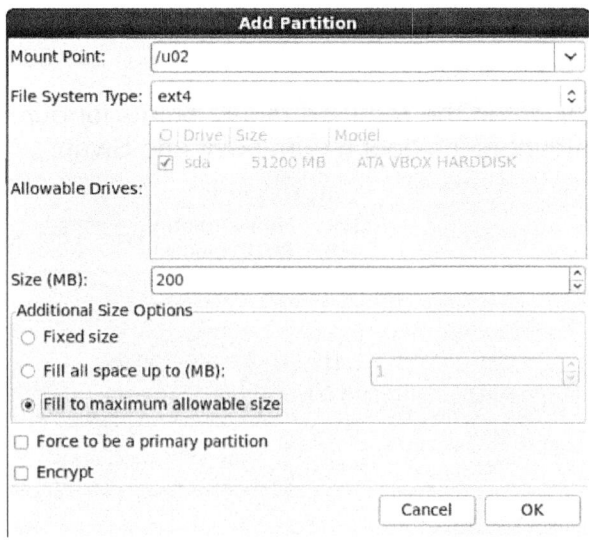

The remaining free space will be allocated to /u02 user mount point. Now we have partitioned our hard disk to multiple file systems.

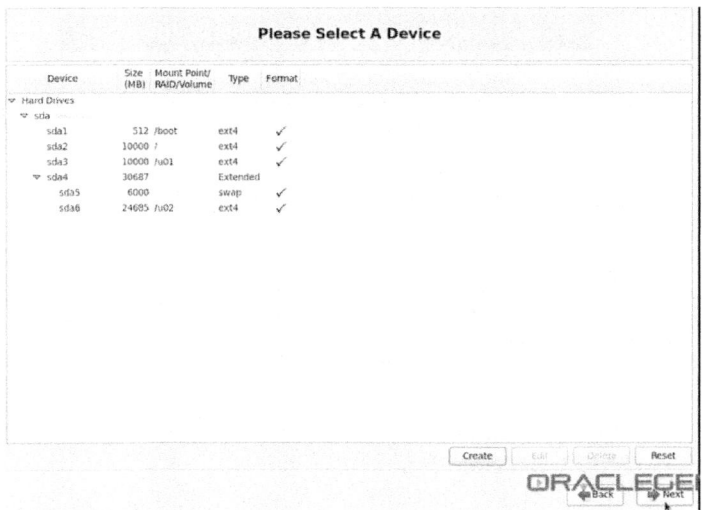

We are now good to go with the installation. Click on Next

A window will pop up where you need to choose the Format option

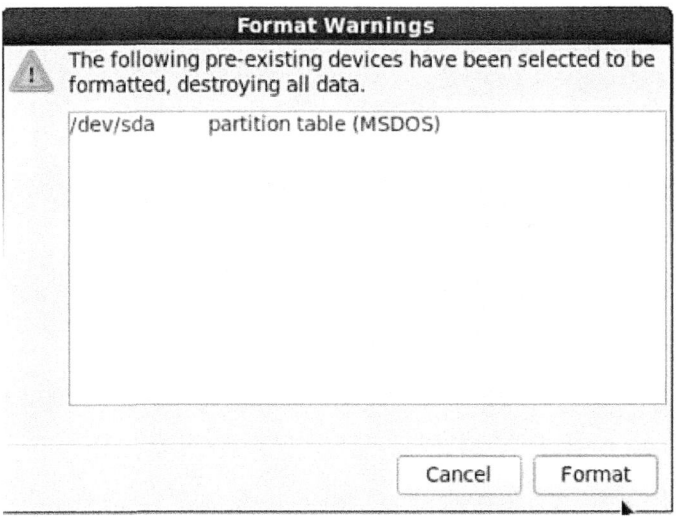

Then choose the option Write changes to disk

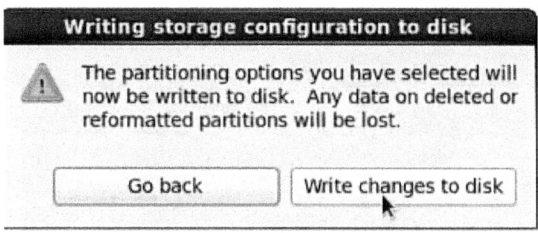

Now all the file systems that you have created will be formatted.

After the format is done, you will get the screen as below. Click on Next button.

Now click on Customize now

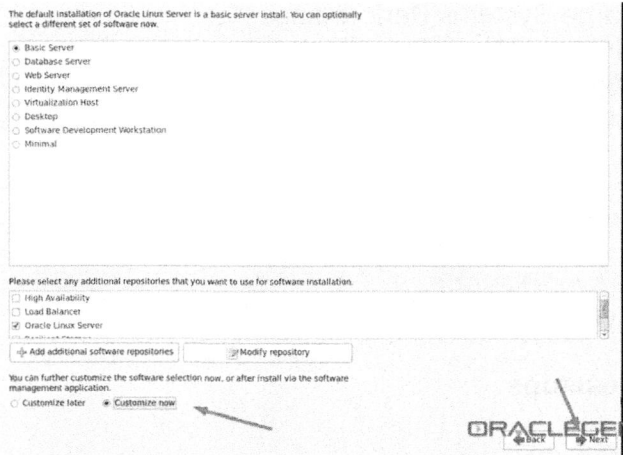

The screen will show some packages that you need to select in order to create your OEL 6.5 server.

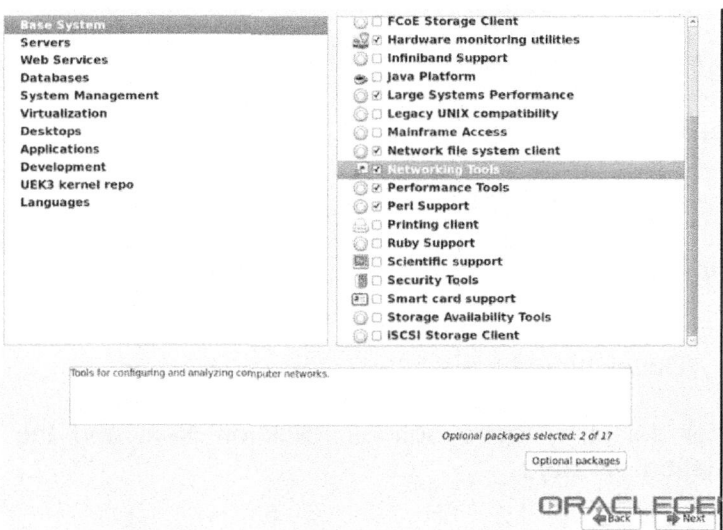

Choose the below mentioned packages:

Under Base System:

- Base
- Compatibility libraries
- Hardware monitoring utilities

- Large Systems Performance
- Network file system client
- Networking tools
- Performance tools
- Perl support

Under Servers:

- Server Platform
- System administration tools

Under Desktops:

- Desktop
- Desktop platform
- Fonts
- General purpose desktop
- Graphical Administration tools
- Input methods
- X Window system

Under Applications:

- Internet Browser

Under Development:

- Additional development
- Development tools

After selecting these options, click on Next and the OEL 6.5 installation will start.

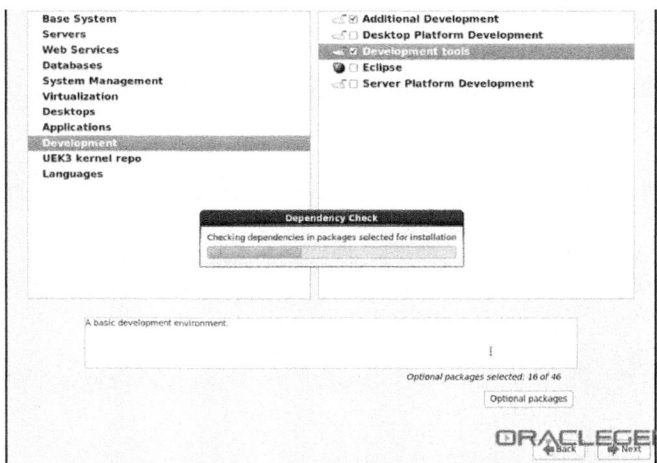

Once the installation is done, installer will prompt you to reboot the machine.

Click on the Reboot button. Then you need to follow some post installation steps which we will learn in the next lesson.

OEL 6.5 Post Installation Steps

After the installation is completed for OEL 6.5, you need to go through some post installation steps.

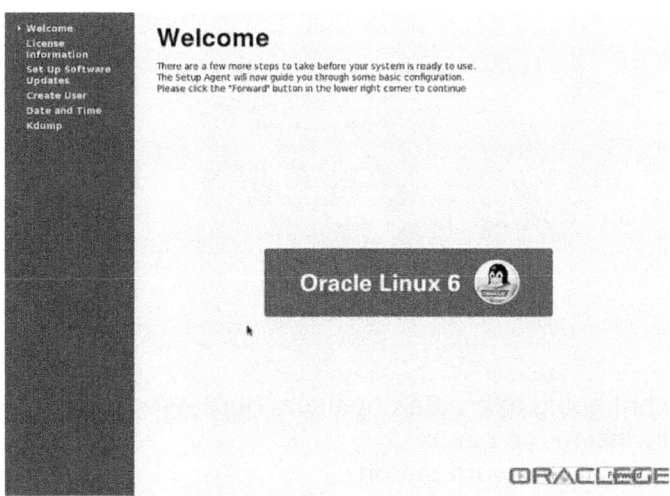

Click on Forward

Accept the license agreement. Click on forward.

Choose "No" in the next screen as you cannot go into Setup software updates.

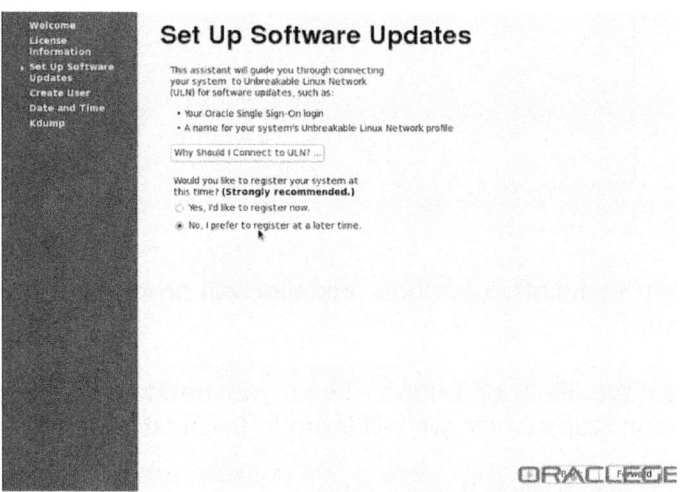

Then click on "No thanks, I'll connect later"

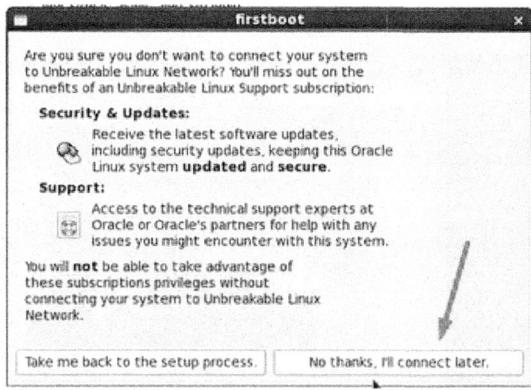

We are not going to create any users here. We will be creating users manually inside the Linux.
So click on the Forward button

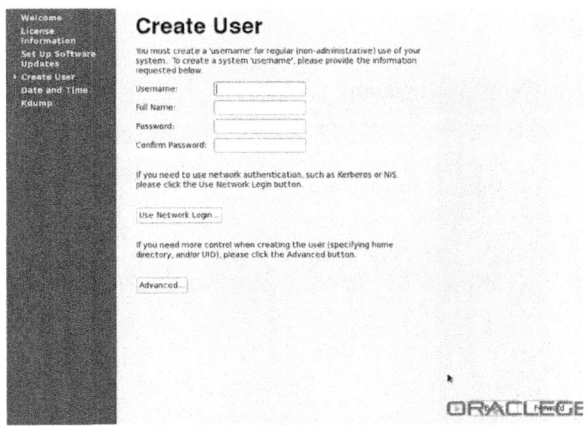

Then a window will pop up, click Yes

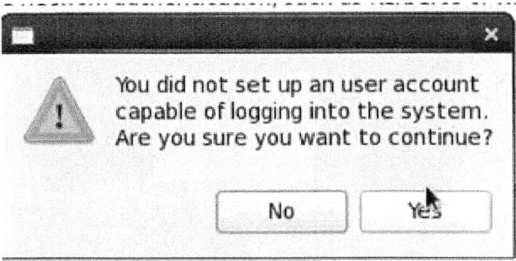

The date and time are already selected. So just click on Forward button.

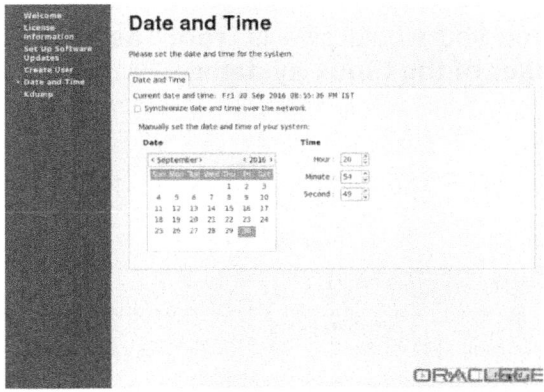

The next screen is Kdump screen. You don't have to do anything here.

Click on Finish

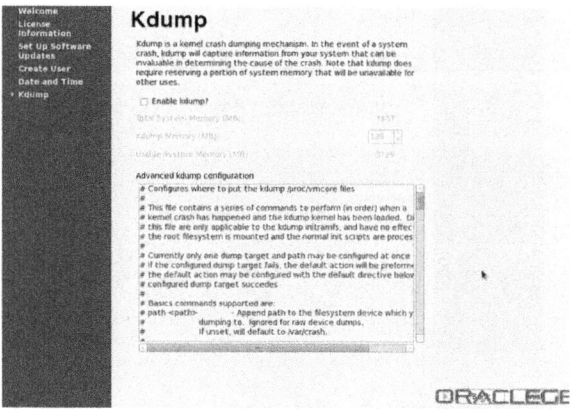

OEL 6.5 installation is done.

Now to login to your system, click on **Other**.

The username you would give is **"root" as root is the master or the super user of the Linux systems.**

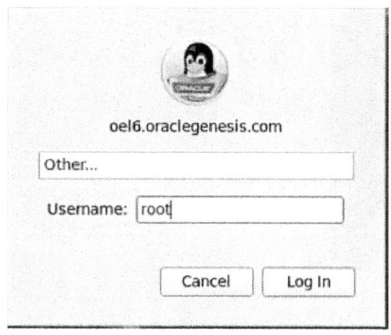

The password would be the one that you gave while installation

Click on Login and you will get a popup on screen.

Choose Do not show me this message again. Then click on Close.

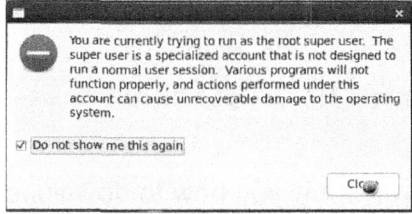

Now the below screenshot is the interface for the OEL 6.5:

## CHAPTER 4

Install CentOS 7 on VirtualBox

Download CentOS 7 ISO file

In this lesson, I will show you how to download the CentOS 7 which is the operating system that we are going to install on the virtual box.

Go to Google.com and type download centos 7

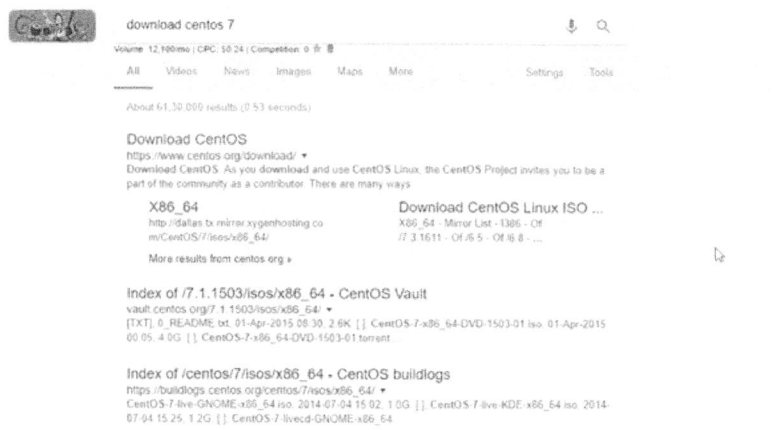

You can click on the first result which is Download CentOS, you will find a window like this below:

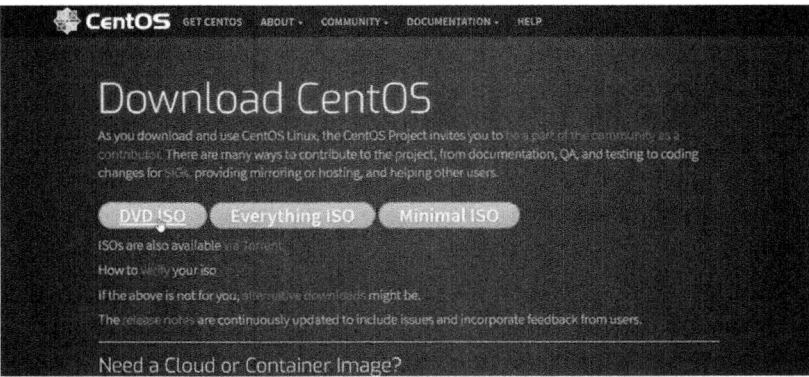

Click on the option DVD ISO

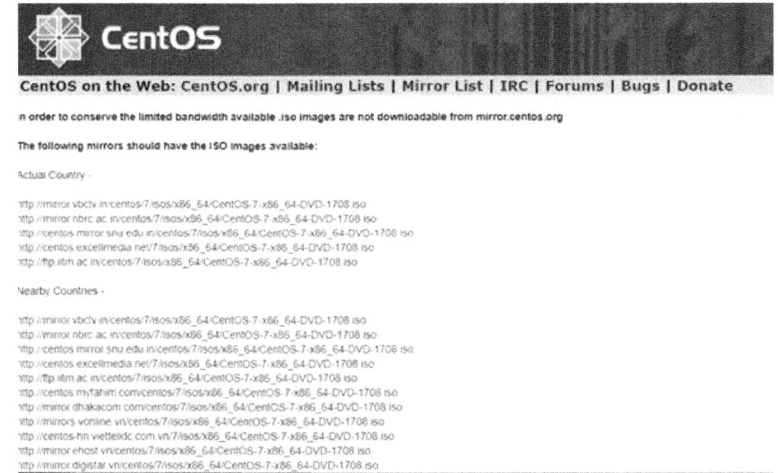

Suppose I want to install an operating system on my laptop, I will insert a CD into the cd drive and then I can boot the system from there.

Unlike the above example of a laptop, a virtual machine does not have a cd drive. Here we have the .iso files which are nothing but the images of the cd drives. We basically feed these images into the virtual machines. So we can use these iso images in place of physical disks because iso images are the copy of the cd disks.

So basically we will boot up the virtual machine using the iso images and eventually we will install the CentOS on the virtual machine.

In the above screenshot, we have lots of links. You can click on any link and download the CentOS software.

One basic reason to download this CentOS software is that we do not have to take the license for this. It is an open source software. You can just download it and practice your Linux learning.

Install CentOS 7 on virtual machine

In this lesson, we will learn to install the CentOS on a newly created virtual machine.

So we will feed the .iso file which we have downloaded into the virtual machine and then we can start the virtual machine.

Right click on the virtual machine

Now click on the Storage option. You can see the virtual cd drive is empty. So we need to load the .iso file that we have downloaded.

We will choose the browse option and click on Choose Virtual optical disk file and locate our file from our local files.

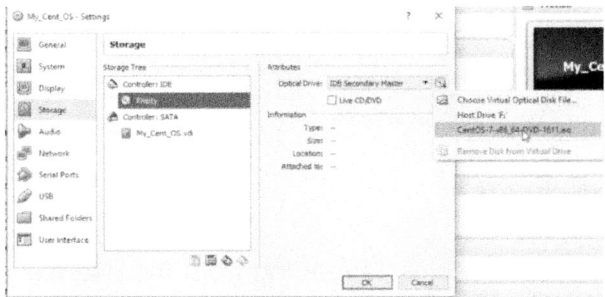

The option for CentOS as an iso file is coming in the above picture as I have already installed it on my system. In your case, you need to browse and locate the file.

Once the .iso file is loaded, click on OK.

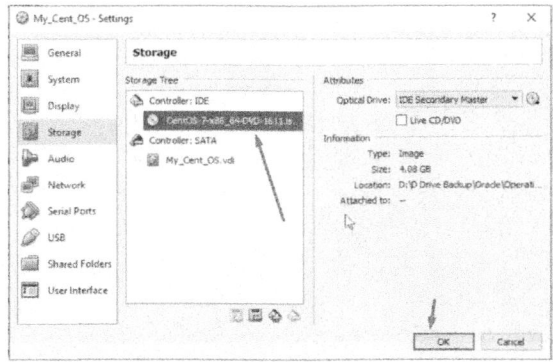

Now we have to install the CentOS installation on the virtual machine.

Click on the Start button after selecting the virtual machine

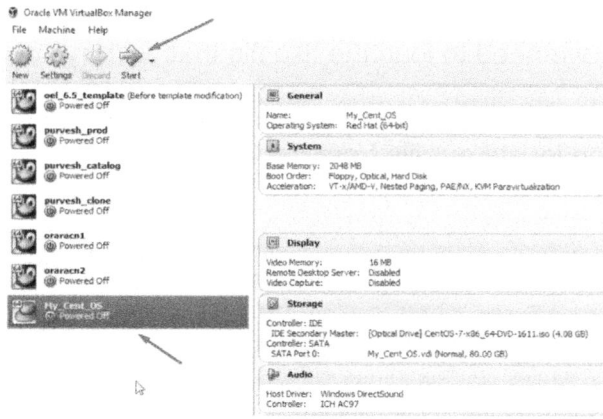

Now the virtual machine is reading from the .iso file and it will start installing the CentOS 7.

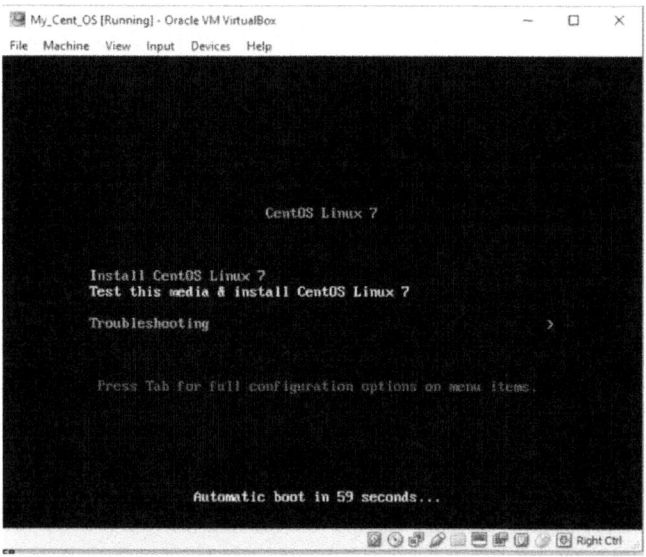

Click inside the virtual machine screen and hit Enter. Once you click inside the virtual machine, the mouse pointer will not show up. To come out of your virtual machine, you need to press the Right Ctrl Key and you can again see mouse pointer.

Now the installation is very simple and straight compared to CentOS 5 or 6.

First screen comes which will ask you to select the Language. Select default language English.

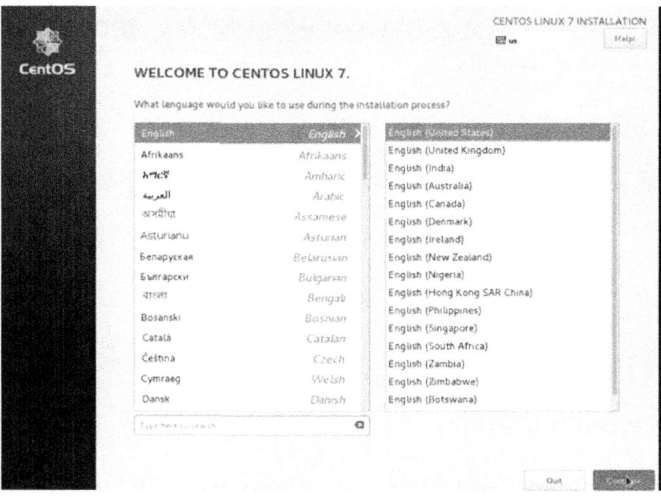

Now the screen comes where some options are seen together.

Date and time will be automatically picked up.

Keyboard language will also be picked up automatically. You already chose the language as English.

Installation Source : If you click on this option, it will show the source from where it will install. You have to do nothing in it.

Software Selection:

- Here we will choose **Server with GUI** under Base Environment on the left hand side.
- On the right hand side, choose **Compatibility Libraries** and **Development Tools** under Add-Ons for Selected Environment.
- Then click on **Done**

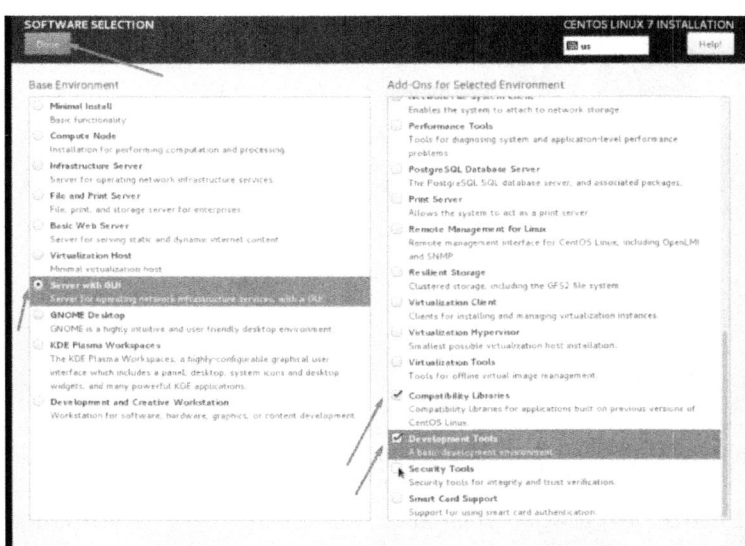

Installation Destination:

This is where CentOS 7 is smart. It will automatically configure the partitioning for you.

In case you are an advanced Linux user, you can configure your own partitioning and choose the option "I will configure partitioning" and click on Done. It will take you to the partitioning screen.

Here we will remain on the option "Automatically configure partitioning" as we will be focusing on only the virtualbox but not learning CentOS administration.

Click on Done.

Kdump:

When you click on Kdump option, you will see that the Kdump option is enabled inside. Sometimes when you are working on Oracle or any other software, you need to disable this option.

So we will remove the tick mark or disable the Kdump option. Then click on Done.

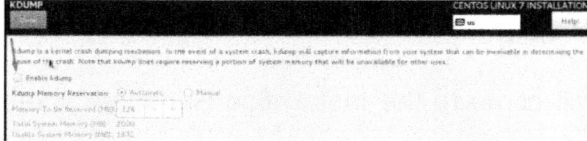

Network & Host name:

Here you can define the network and host name for the machine.

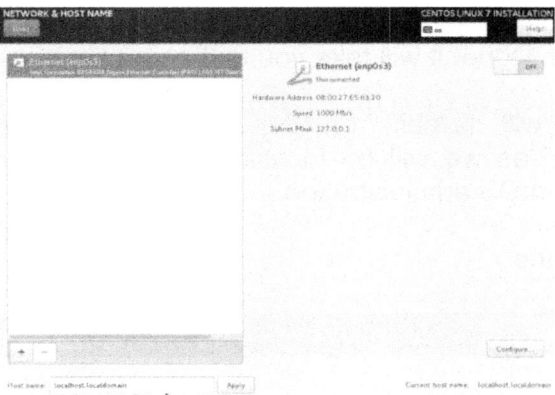

We will assign a host name as mycentos.

Then we will enable the network. Just click on the button beside Ethernet (enpOs3) to ON from OFF and click on Configure button to allocate an IP address to this virtual machine.

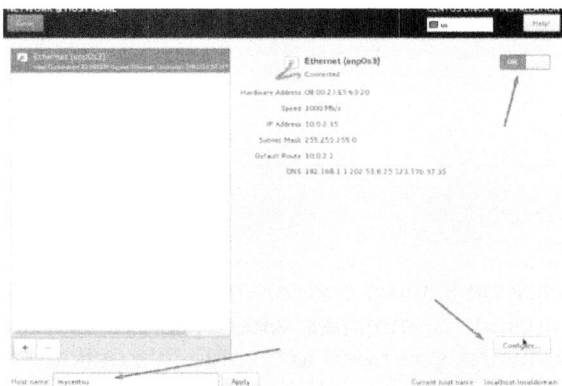

But here we will Cancel the Network setup right now as we will do it manually once the installation is done.

So just click on Done.

Now we will come to the Installation Summary screen and we will click on **Begin Installation.**

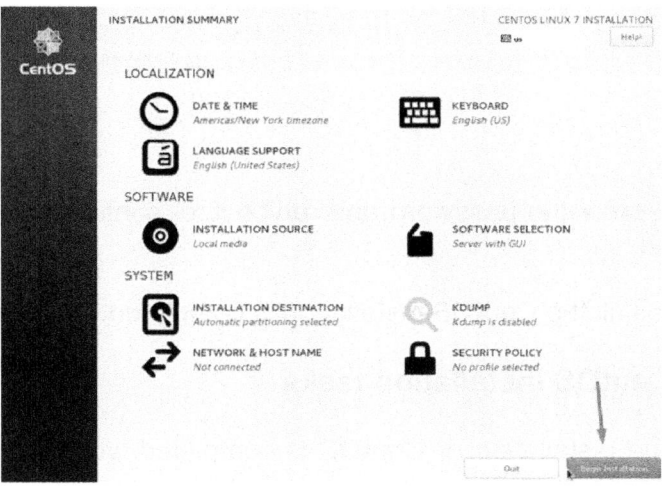

It will start installing the CentOS.

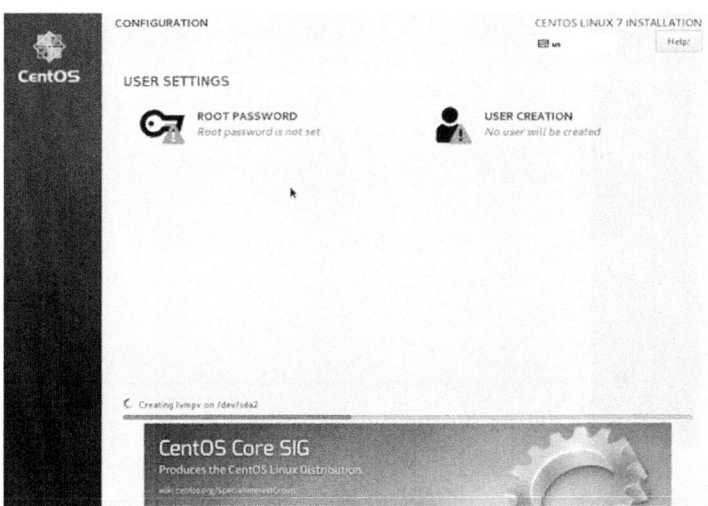

Meanwhile we will set the Root password by clicking on ROOT PASSWORD.

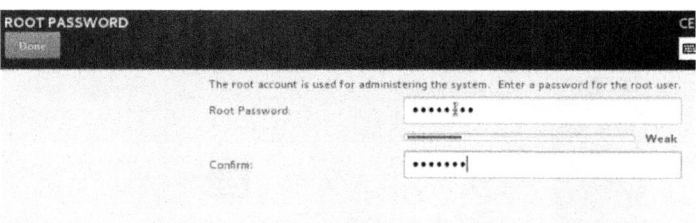

We will enter the password and retype it for confirmation. Then click on Done.

Now wait till the CentOS installation is completed.

Post CentOS installation tasks

Once the installation of CentOS is completed, you need to click on the Reboot button.

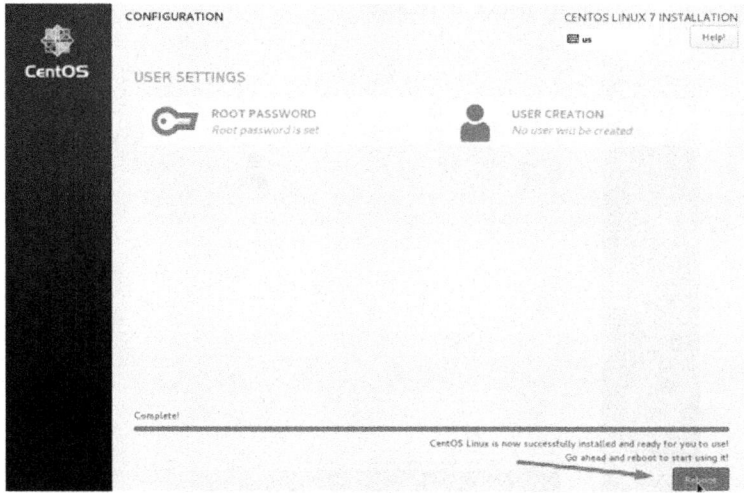

It will not reboot the windows operating system. It will only reboot the virtual machine.

Now it will restart the virtual machine and automatically the CentOS startup screen will come up where we need to set some settings.

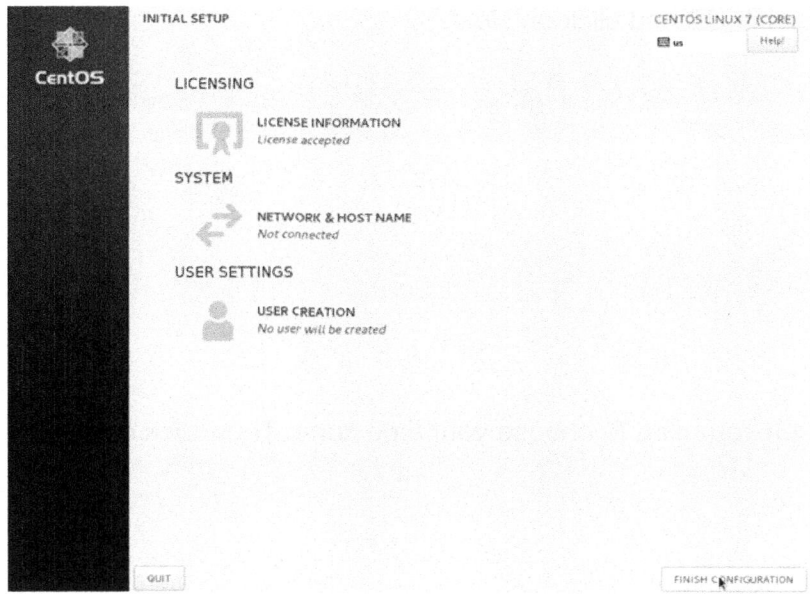

Click on the License Information and then Accept it. Then click on Done.

Then just click on "Finish Configuration"

This will bring up the screen with some options to choose for us.

We will choose English and click on Next.

Then it will ask you to choose the keyboard language. Choose

English US and click on Next.

Then you need to choose your time zone. Then click on Next.

Now it will ask you to Connect with your online accounts. I will choose Skip here for now.

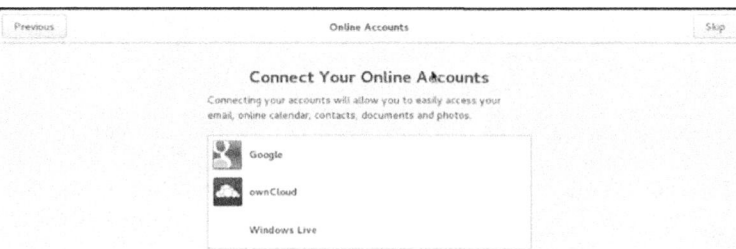

Then it would force you to create at least one user. So create a user name. Then click on Next

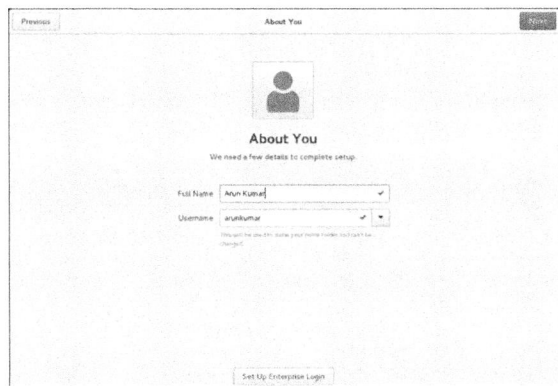

Now it will ask you the Password. Enter and confirm and then click on Next.

Now we are done with the setup also.

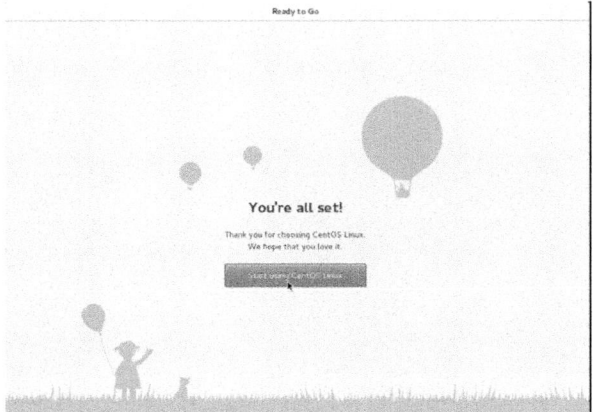

Now you can click on Start using CentOS Linux. For the first time, the screen will appear which will help you in getting started.

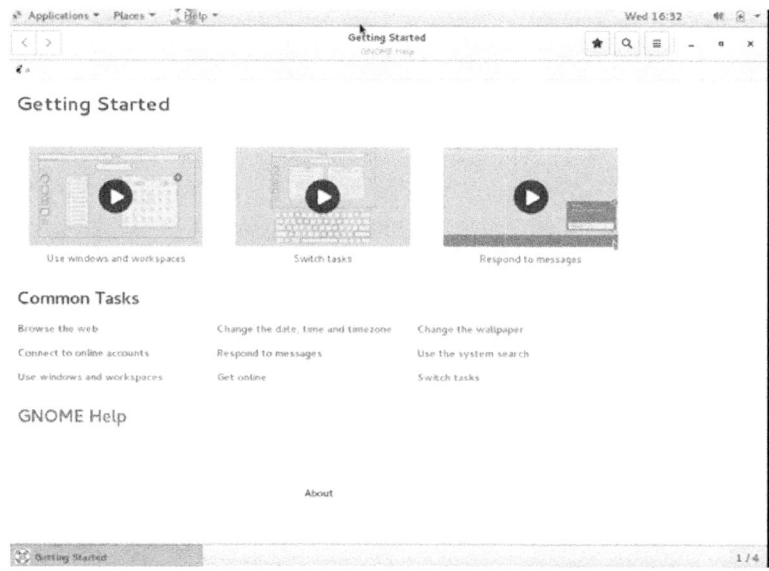

When you are done with it, close it. Then you can see your CentOS 7 Desktop on screen.

Setup Network for CentOS machine

In the previous lesson, we learnt to set up the post installation steps for CentOS 7. In this lesson, we will understand how to assign an IP address to our virtual machine.

If you don't assign the IP address to a virtual machine, you won't be able to communicate to the virtual machine over the network.

Before we assign the IP address to the virtual machine, we need to get the IP address of our windows system or our own host system.

First we need to go to cmd (command prompt) on our system.

Type **ipconfig** under your command prompt.

As I am connected to a Wi-Fi netwrok, I would look under Wireless Lan adapter Wi-Fi. If you are connected with a ethernet connection, you need to look under Ethernet adapter.

My system IP address is

IPv4 Address: 192.168.0.90
Subnet Mask: 255.255.255.0
Default Gateway: 192.168.0.1

So now the question **is how you can decide the IP address for your virtual machine?**

- In the above case, my system IP address is 192.168.0.90. So I cannot assign the same IP address to any other machine in my network.
- The first three parts of the host system IP address will be the same for any other machine on the same network. So the first 3 parts of the virtual machine should be 192.168.0.---.
- The last part or value should be always between 0 and 255 but never should be 90(which is our system host IP).
- Never assign the last value of the IP address between 0 to 10. Always go for a very high value because your system automatically dynamically assigns these small numbers or initial numbers to the other machines that are connected to the network (mobile phones, tabs, other systems or laptops at your home). It is recommended that you give a value between 50 to 255. This is a safe range for us so that the virtual machine IP does not clash with other assigned IPs.

So after having all the above points in mind, we will take the IP address as 192.168.0.93

Now comes the Subnet Mask. It would remain the same as the host system. So it would be 255.255.255.0

Gateway IP is nothing but the router IP. So it will also be the same as all the machines will communicate to each other and internet via the router. So the Default Gateway will be 192.168.0.1.

So the IP address is ready now for the virtual machine. Now we will get inside the CentOS virtual machine.

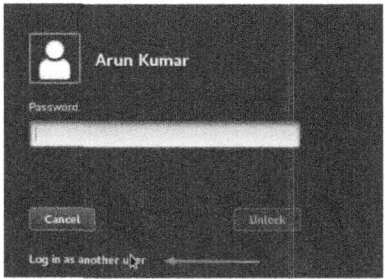

We need to login with the "root" user but not with the normal user that we have created earlier. So click on "Log in as another user".

Click on Not listed? Then it will ask for the username and password.

Give the Username as "root"

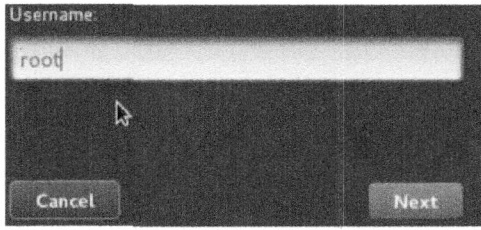

Click on Next and give the Password.

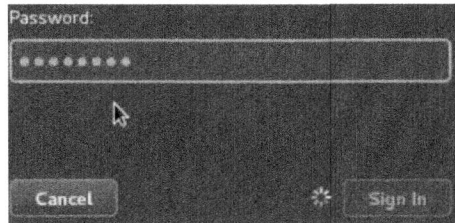

So, all the network level changes and other changes are done via the "root" user in general.

It will ask for some options to select once again for the first time we log in. You need to choose the language and keyboard language. Then click on Start using CentOS Linux.

On the CentOS desktop, you need to click on the small arrow like button on the extreme right up corner of the screen.

Then a window will open where you will see "**Wired**". This is nothing but the network that we have.

Under Wired, you need to click on **Wired settings**.

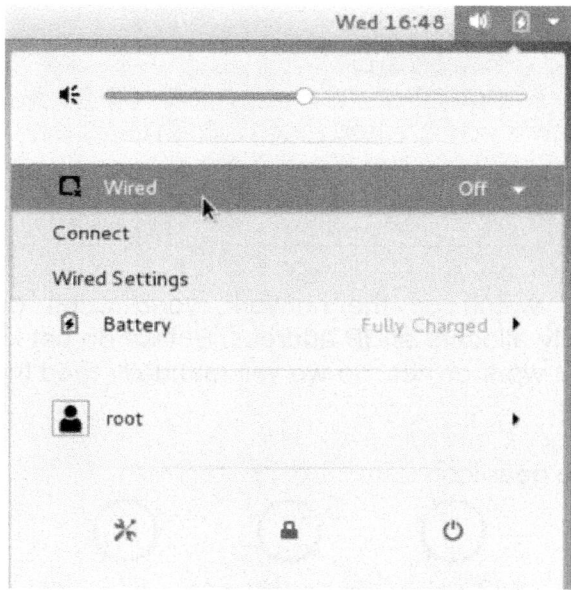

When you click on Wired Settings, a window will open:

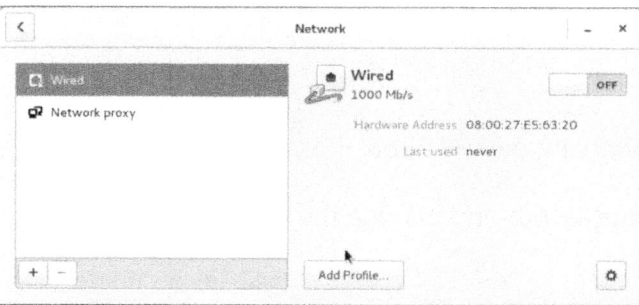

You can see above that we did not set up any network for this machine.

So we will switch ON the network by clicking on the OFF button on the right hand corner of the window.

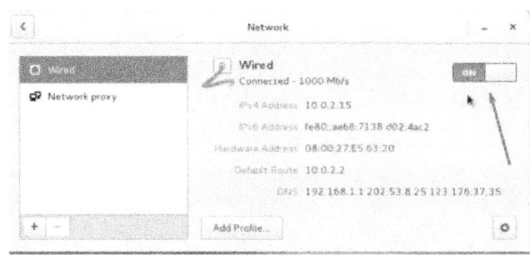

When you switch on the network, your router or machine will automatically allocate an IP address. But we do not know that the IP address will work or not. So we will manually feed the IP address in the network.

Click on the gear icon

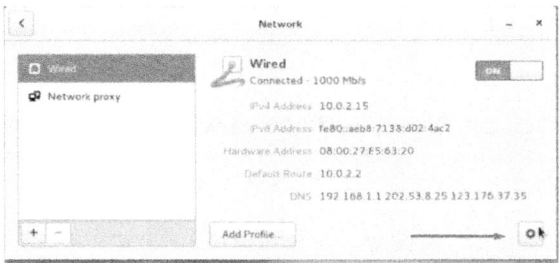

Now a new window will open.

Go to **Identity** tab and choose the option **Connect automatically**

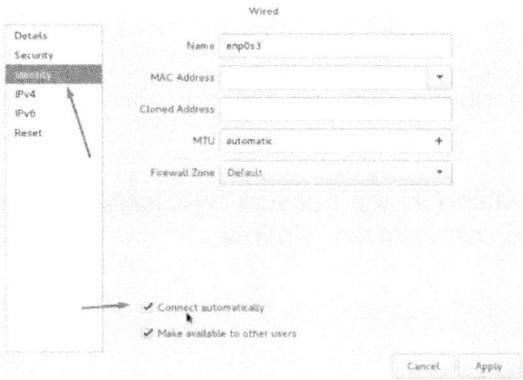

Then come to the IPv4 tab and select the Addreses as Manual in place of Automatic (default) as you are going to feed the IP address to the virtually machine manually.

When you select the Manual option, it will ask for the IP address. So now you need to feed the IP address that we decided earlier.

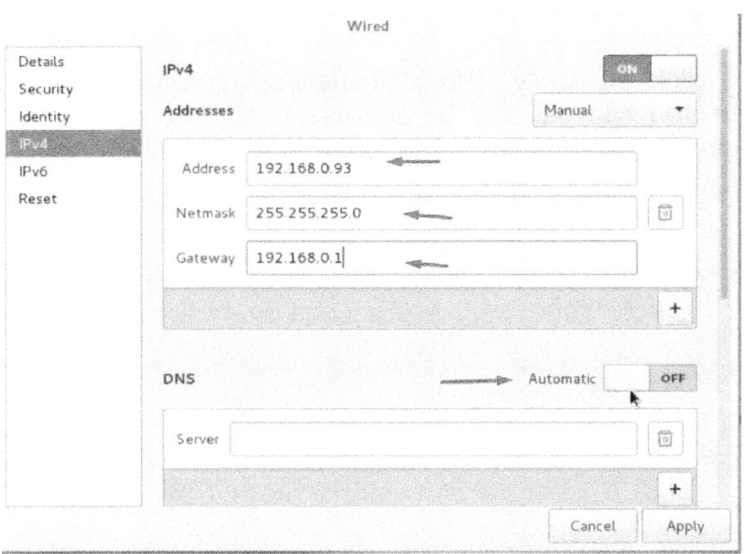

IP address : 192.168.0.93
Subnet mask : 255.255.255.0

Gatweway : 192.168.0.1

We need to switch OFF the DNS option as shown above.

When we scroll down, we will get option for Routes. We will switch it OFF as well.

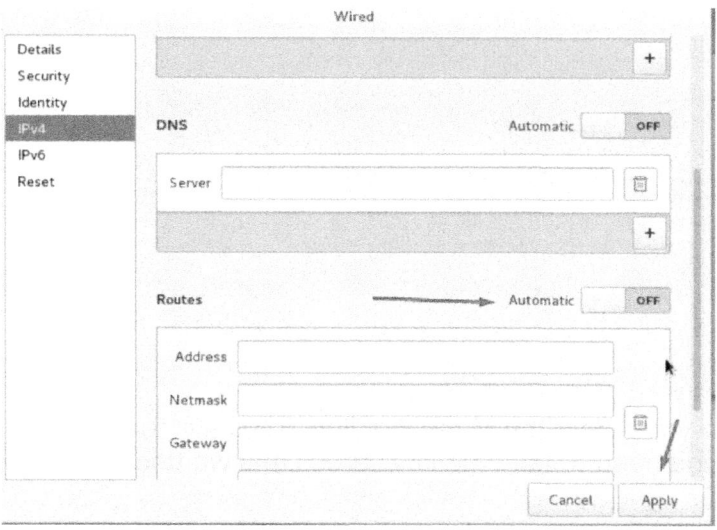

Then click on Apply. The Main network screen will appear again where you can see the IP address is still the old one which was assigned by the system or the router automatically.

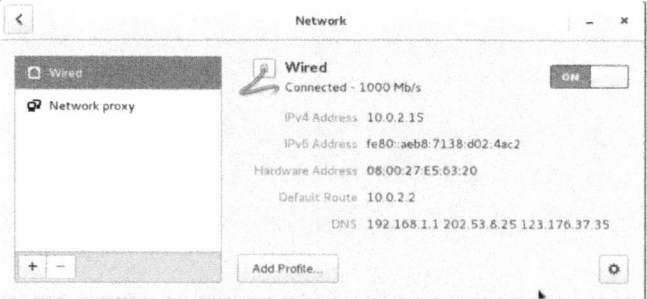

So we will switch OFF the network and again switch it ON.

Now you can see the IP address is changed to what we have assigned.

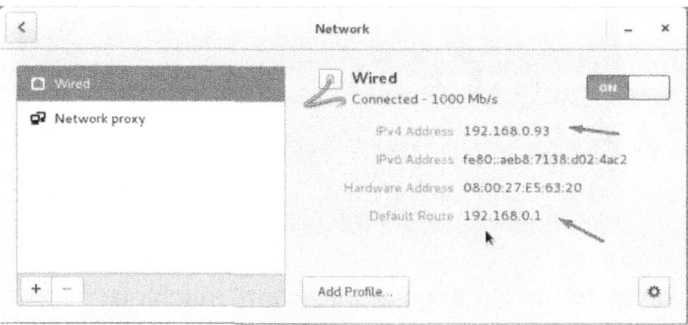

IP address under IPv4 Address: 192.168.0.93
Default Gateway under Default Route: 192.168.0.1

So now that we have assigned the IP address, we would check whether we can ping the virtual machine in the command prompt or we would check whether our host system is able to communicate with the virtual machine or not.

So I will ping the IP address in windows cmd prompt.

When I ping the IP address, it is showing me that the IP is unreachable.

```
Tunnel adapter Local Area Connection* 11:

   Media State . . . . . . . . . . . : Media disconnected
   Connection-specific DNS Suffix  . :

C:\Users\aksgolu>
C:\Users\aksgolu>
C:\Users\aksgolu>
C:\Users\aksgolu>ping 192.168.0.93

Pinging 192.168.0.93 with 32 bytes of data:
Reply from 192.168.0.90: Destination host unreachable.
Reply from 192.168.0.90: Destination host unreachable.
```

Now I will go to the Settings of the virtual machine

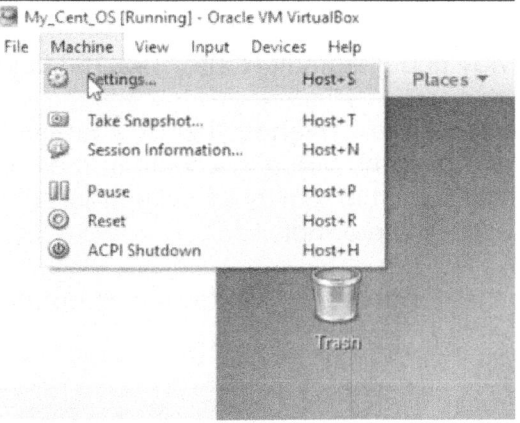

In Settings, we need to go to Network.

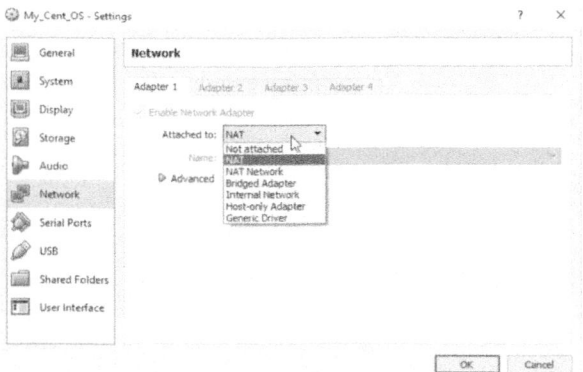

Then Select Bridged Adapter in the drop down menu of "Attached to:"

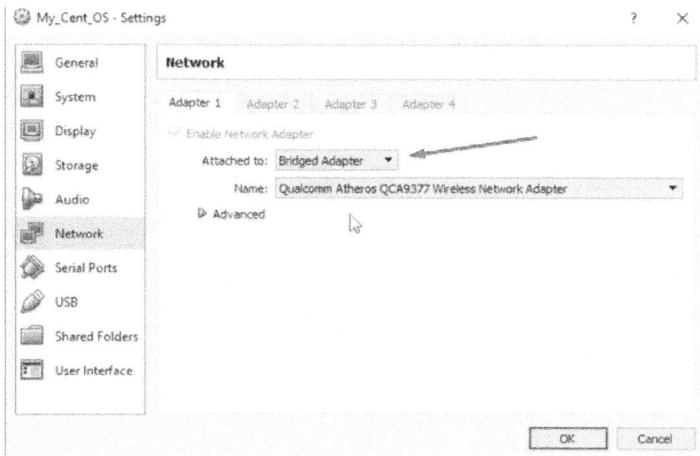

Click on Ok button.

Now if you try to Ping in windows cmd prompt, you will get the response which means it will connect to the virtual machine.

So this is how you set up the network for any Linux virtual machine.

We can also check this via PuTTY. We will give the IP address 192.168.0.93 in the host name in PuTTY.

105

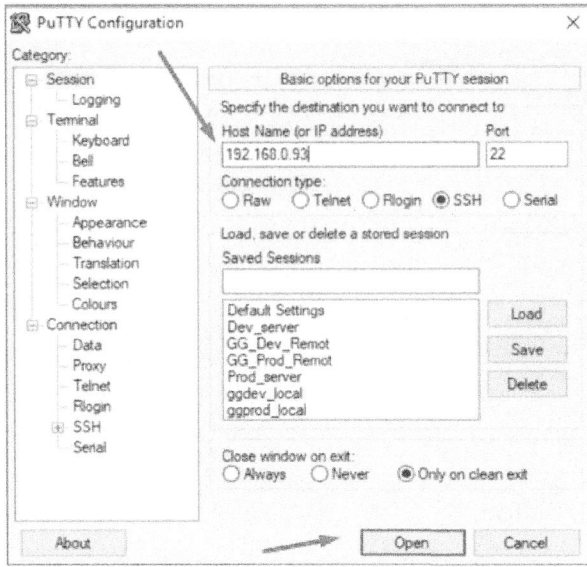

It will connect to the virtual machine "mycentOS"

In the above case, we have connected to the IP address. Then we gave the root username and the password for it. It got connected to the hostname "my CentOS".

## CHAPTER 5

Must know VirtualBox Administration

Increase Virtual Machine RAM

In the last lesson, we have learnt how to set up network for our CentOS machine.

Now that the networking is set, we will learn about how to increase or decrease the RAM allocated to this virtual machine.

Suppose you are working on a virtual machine and you find the memory of the system is very low. For instance, we have assigned 2GB to the virtual machine my CentOS.

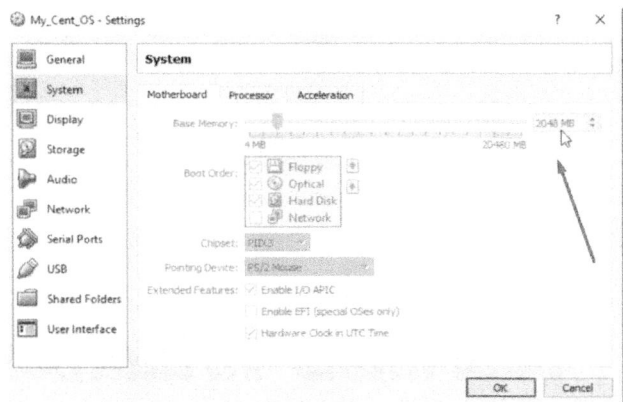

Suppose you want to increase the RAM size of the above machine as you want to install some programs or applications on this virtual machine. You need to allocate more memory from your windows machine to this virtual machine.

So close the virtual machine first and go to the virtualbox manager.

Select and right click on the last machine (My_Cent_OS) and go to the settings

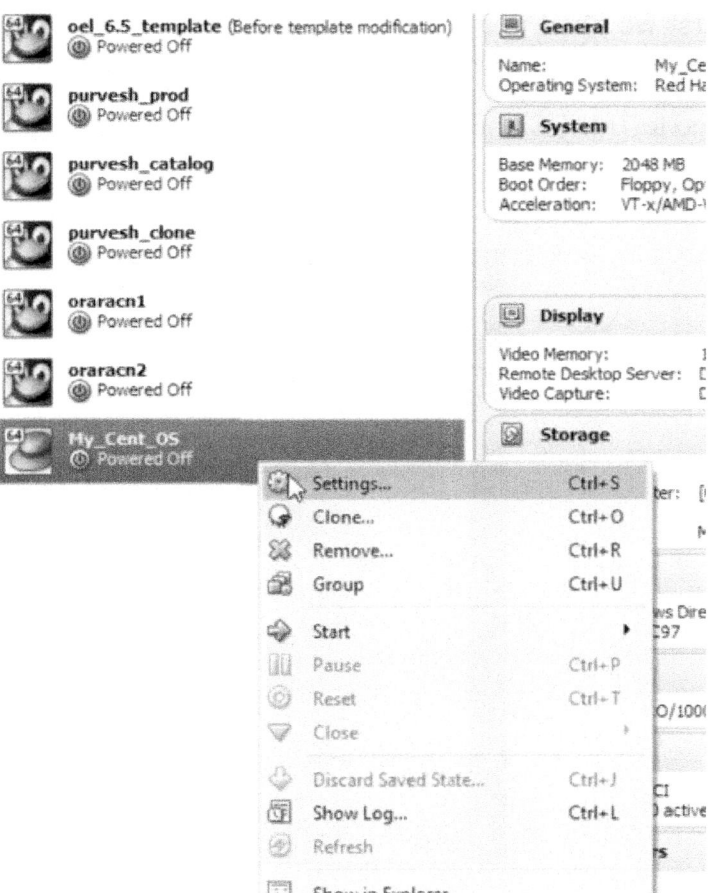

Now the slider is enabled to increase or decrease the RAM.

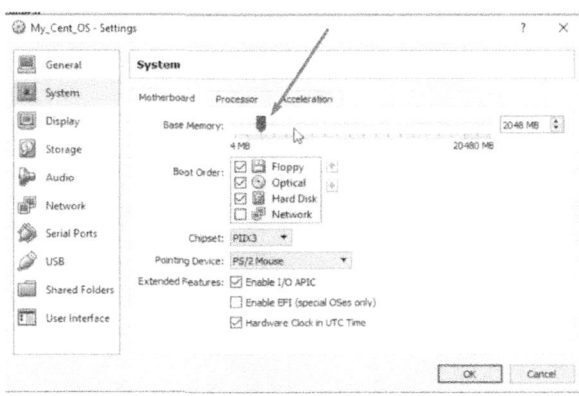

But first we need to calculate the amount of memory that we have on our windows machine.

I will go to This PC and right click on it.

Then go to Properties.

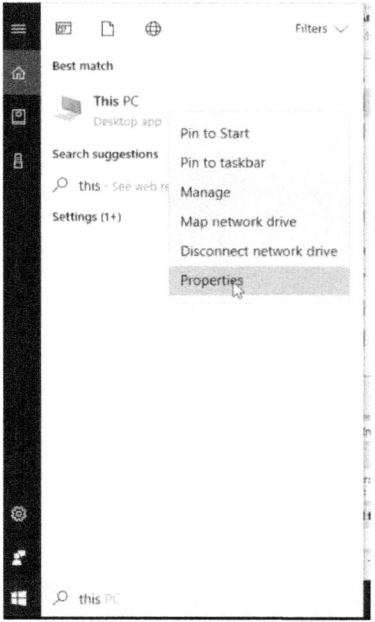

Now the screen will show how much memory is there on my PC.

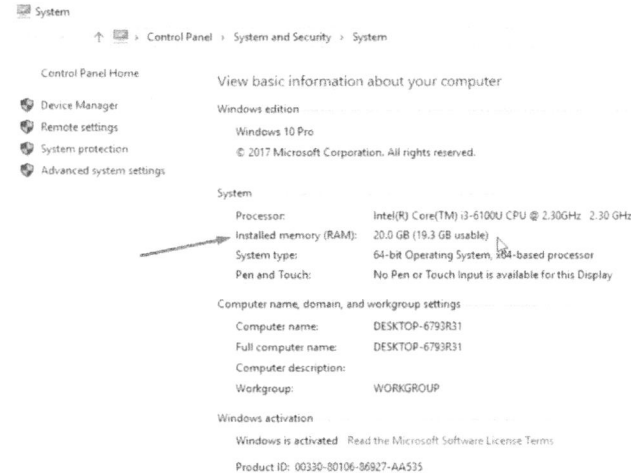

On my PC, there is 20GB of RAM as shown in the above screenshot. But I cannot allocate entire 20GB to the virtual machine as the windows operating system also needs some memory to run. Also on windows, there are other programs that are running which you can see in the task bar. So each program requires some memory to run.

So we should never try to allocate the entire memory to a virtual machine as windows operating system will become slow. So if your host OS (windows in this case) is getting slow, then your guest OS or the virtual machine will also become slow even if you have lot of RAM in your virtual machine.

So, a thumb rule for the above case is always keep 4 to 5 GB of RAM for your windows OS to run.

We will increase the RAM size of the virtual machine to 4GB from 2GB.

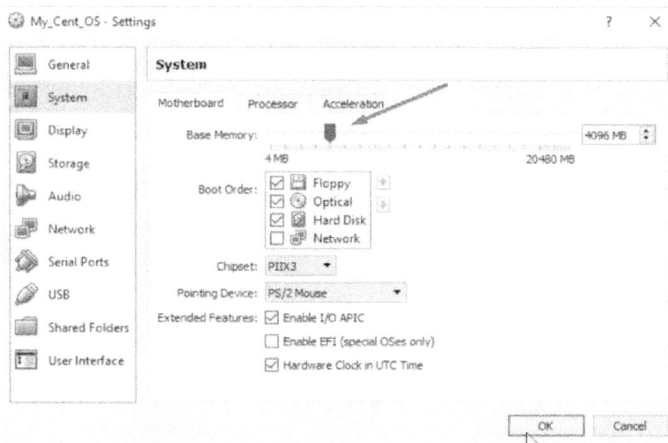

Remember:

The memory allocation will not happen immediately after you assign the RAM (increase the RAM). It will happen when you start the virtual machine.

Suppose all the virtual machines are powered off now. Windows can utilize the whole 20 GB to run itself and its programs and applications. But when you start the virtual machine which is now having the RAM as 4GB, windows will take only 16 GB to run.

So RAM will be consumed only when the virtual machine is running.

Add new disk to Virtual Machine

In the last lesson, we learnt how to increase or decrease the RAM for a virtual machine.

In this lesson, we will learn how to add the hard disk space to a virtual machine.

Suppose we have a new directory /apps and you want to allocate 100 GB to this directory. We have only 80 GB in our virtual machine which also contains the Operating system and some more software. First of all, it is impossible to allocate 100 GB out of 80 GB.

The only solution is to add a new hard disk to your virtual machine. Once the hard disk is added, we will learn how we can mount that 100 GB hard disk on /apps.

First of all, make sure your virtual machine is down or powered off.

Go to Settings

In settings, go to the Storage option.

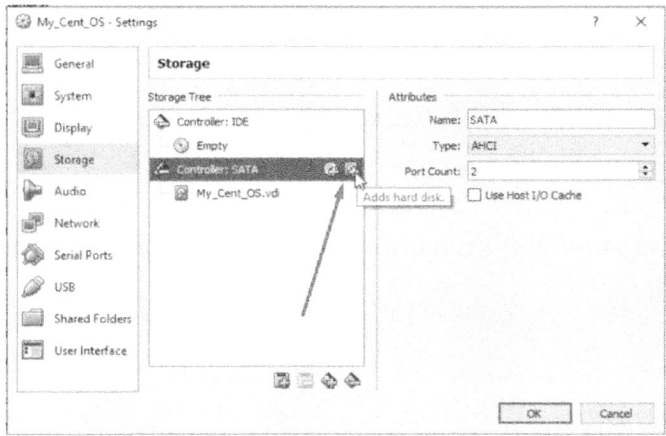

You can see the highlighted option for **Controller: SATA**. Beside the SATA controller, you have a button which Adds hard disk as shown in the above screenshot.

Click on the Adds hard disk button

You will get a window where you need to select Create new disk.

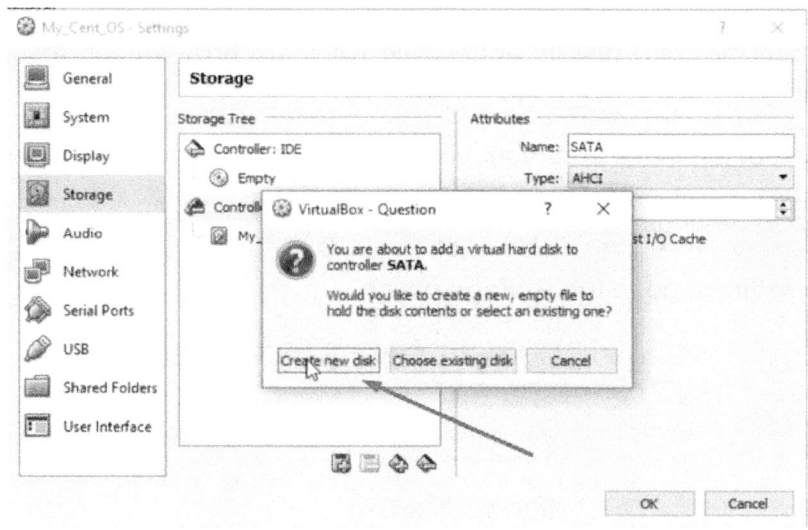

Then choose VDI (Virtualbox disk image) option. Click Next

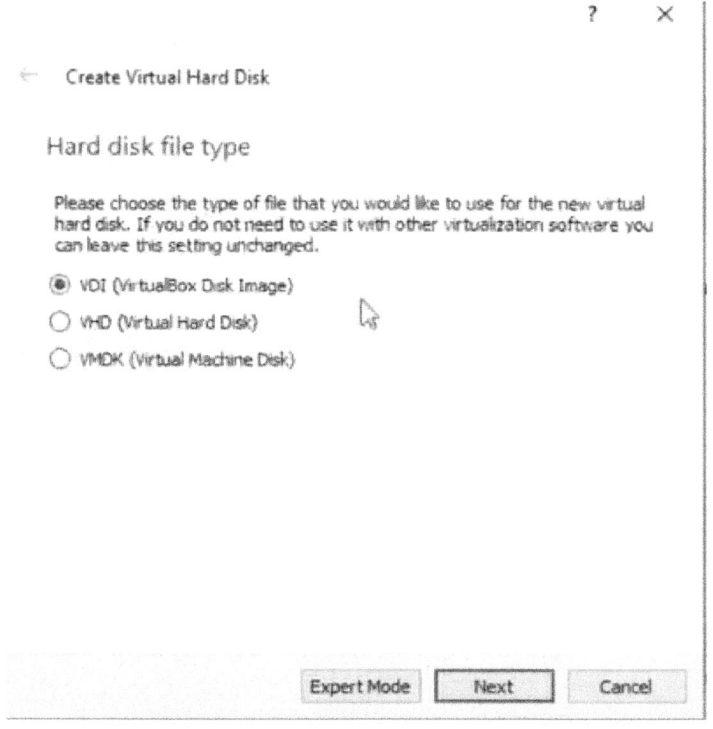

Then choose Dynamically allocated option in the next screen and click on Next.

Now give a name to this disk as HDD_4_APP and allocate 100GB to the hard disk.

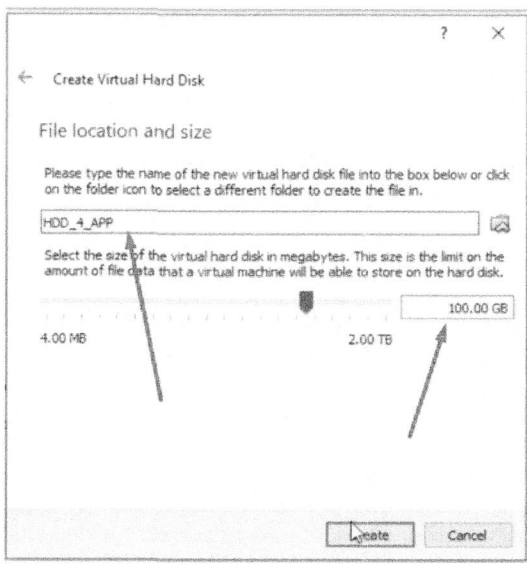

Then click on Create.

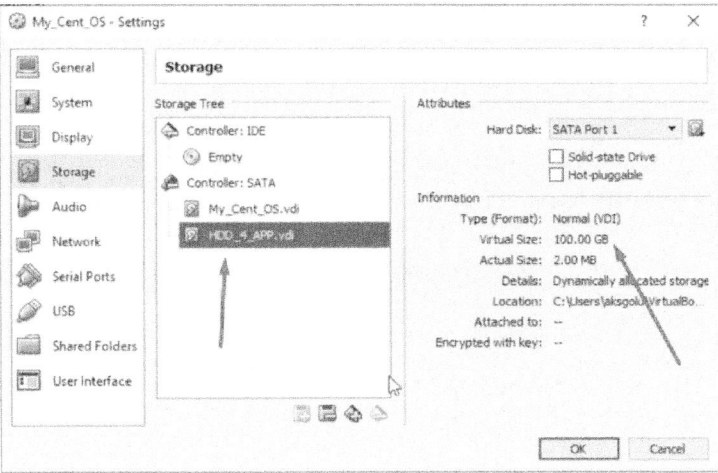

Now click on OK button.

Now let us first discuss the steps we will follow here:

1. Add new HDD at VM level
2. Format the new HDD → create partitions
3. Create filesystem on the partition
4. Create /apps directory
5. Mount new HDD on apps
6. Add the directory mount under /etc/fstab

We have already completed the 1st step which is to add new HDD at VM level. Now we need to format the hard disk.

So first get inside the virtual machine and login as root user.

Enter the username root

Then enter the password.

Now VM is up and running. Now open a new terminal

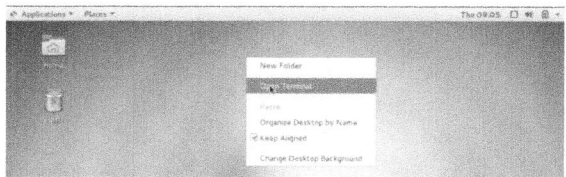

Now type fdisk -l

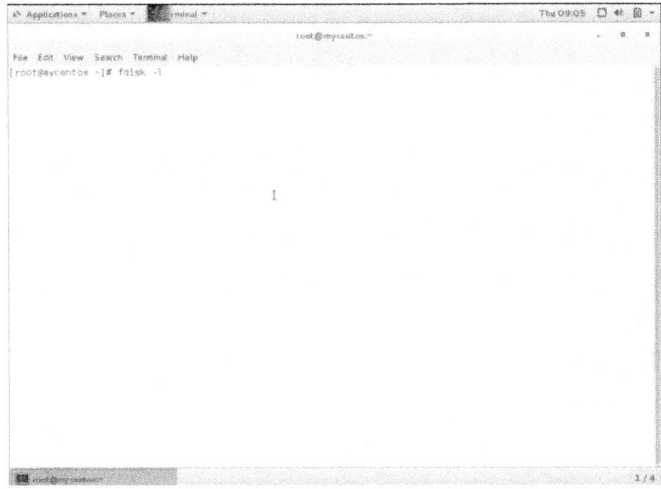

fdisk -l is a format disk utility that helps you to format hard disk within the Linux operating system.

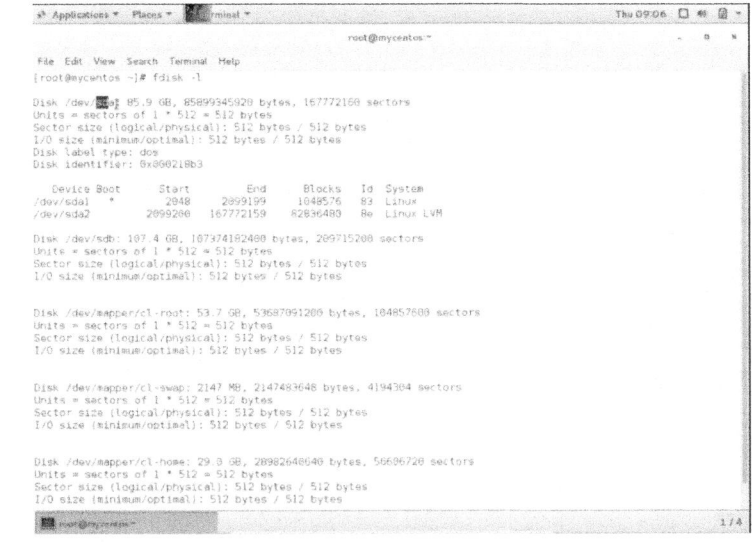

In the above screenshot, you have Disk /dev/sda.

In sda, sd is nothing but storage device and 'a' is the name assigned to the disk. You will also see sdb in the down. So sdb is storage device b.

The size of the disk a is around 85 GB here and the size of the disk b is about 107 GB. You might be thinking by now that we have assigned only 80 GB but it is 85 GB here. The reason is the Linux counts the GB in a little bit smaller sectors and cylinders than what windows count the GBs.

Now we need to format the disk-b. We will type fdisk /dev/sdb

fdisk /dev/sdb command will allow you to format the disk.

If you type m, it will show all the listed commands.

- After formatting, we will type n for creating a new partition.
- We will choose p for the primary partition type.
- Partition number would be 1
- First sector- We will go with the default one
- Last sector- We will go with the default one
- Now we just need to type w which will save the partition table.

We are going with the default size because we want to create only one partition for the entire 107GB space. **You can hit Enter for selecting the default one.**

```
Command (m for help): n
Partition type:
    p   primary (0 primary, 0 extended, 4 free)
    e   extended
Select (default p): p
Partition number (1-4, default 1): 1
First sector (2048-209715199, default 2048):
Using default value 2048
Last sector, +sectors or +size{K,M,G} (2048-209715199, default 209715199):
Using default value 209715199
Partition 1 of type Linux and of size 100 GiB is set

Command (m for help): w
The partition table has been altered!

Calling ioctl() to re-read partition table.
Syncing disks.
[root@mycentos ~]#
[root@mycentos ~]#          I
```

Now if you type fdisk -l /dev/sdb and hit enter, it will show that one partition is created in the disk b as in /dev/sdb1 and the partition is of size around 107 GB.

```
Command (m for help): w
The partition table has been altered!

Calling ioctl() to re-read partition table.
Syncing disks.
[root@mycentos ~]#
[root@mycentos ~]#
[root@mycentos ~]#
[root@mycentos ~]# fdisk -l /dev/sdb

Disk /dev/sdb: 107.4 GB, 107374182400 bytes, 209715200 sectors
Units = sectors of 1 * 512 = 512 bytes
Sector size (logical/physical): 512 bytes / 512 bytes
I/O size (minimum/optimal): 512 bytes / 512 bytes
Disk label type: dos
Disk identifier: 0x6e0b2e78

   Device Boot      Start         End      Blocks   Id  System
/dev/sdb1            2048   209715199   104856576   83  Linux
[root@mycentos ~]#
[root@mycentos ~]#
```

Now we need to define the file system for the disk.

We will type mkfs.xfs /dev/sdb1 and hit enter.

Here mkfs is the command and xfs is the file system. You can just remember this storage command.

```
Disk /dev/sdb: 107.4 GB, 107374182400 bytes, 209715200 sectors
Units = sectors of 1 * 512 = 512 bytes
Sector size (logical/physical): 512 bytes / 512 bytes
I/O size (minimum/optimal): 512 bytes / 512 bytes
Disk label type: dos
Disk identifier: 0x6e0b2e78

   Device Boot      Start         End      Blocks   Id  System
/dev/sdb1             2048   209715199   104856576   83  Linux
[root@mycentos ~]#
[root@mycentos ~]#
[root@mycentos ~]#
[root@mycentos ~]# mkfs.xfs /dev/sdb1
meta-data=/dev/sdb1              isize=512    agcount=4, agsize=6553536 blks
         =                       sectsz=512   attr=2, projid32bit=1
         =                       crc=1        finobt=0, sparse=0
data     =                       bsize=4096   blocks=26214144, imaxpct=25
         =                       sunit=0      swidth=0 blks
naming   =version 2              bsize=4096   ascii-ci=0 ftype=1
log      =internal log           bsize=4096   blocks=12799, version=2
         =                       sectsz=512   sunit=0 blks, lazy-count=1
realtime =none                   extsz=4096   blocks=0, rtextents=0
[root@mycentos ~]#
[root@mycentos ~]#
[root@mycentos ~]#
[root@mycentos ~]# █
```

So you can see above that Linux has formatted the sdb1 as xfs file system. Now our job is to make the directory /apps.

So we will give the command mkdir /apps

```
   Device Boot      Start         End      Blocks   Id  System
/dev/sdb1             2048   209715199   104856576   83  Linux
[root@mycentos ~]#
[root@mycentos ~]#
[root@mycentos ~]#
[root@mycentos ~]# mkfs.xfs /dev/sdb1
meta-data=/dev/sdb1              isize=512    agcount=4, agsize=6553536 blks
         =                       sectsz=512   attr=2, projid32bit=1
         =                       crc=1        finobt=0, sparse=0
data     =                       bsize=4096   blocks=26214144, imaxpct=25
         =                       sunit=0      swidth=0 blks
naming   =version 2              bsize=4096   ascii-ci=0 ftype=1
log      =internal log           bsize=4096   blocks=12799, version=2
         =                       sectsz=512   sunit=0 blks, lazy-count=1
realtime =none                   extsz=4096   blocks=0, rtextents=0
[root@mycentos ~]#
[root@mycentos ~]#
[root@mycentos ~]#
[root@mycentos ~]#
[root@mycentos ~]# mkdir /apps
mkdir: cannot create directory '/apps': File exists
[root@mycentos ~]#
[root@mycentos ~]#
[root@mycentos ~]#
[root@mycentos ~]# █
```

In the above screenshot, the /apps directory is already there. This is the reason it is showing /apps already exists.

We will directly mount it on the /apps directory. So we will check where it is mounted.

```
[root@mycentos ~]# mkfs.xfs /dev/sdb1
meta-data=/dev/sdb1                isize=512    agcount=4, agsize=6553536 blks
         =                         sectsz=512   attr=2, projid32bit=1
         =                         crc=1        finobt=0, sparse=0
data     =                         bsize=4096   blocks=26214144, imaxpct=25
         =                         sunit=0      swidth=0 blks
naming   =version 2               bsize=4096   ascii-ci=0 ftype=1
log      =internal log            bsize=4096   blocks=12799, version=2
         =                         sectsz=512   sunit=0 blks, lazy-count=1
realtime =none                    extsz=4096   blocks=0, rtextents=0
[root@mycentos ~]#
[root@mycentos ~]#
[root@mycentos ~]#
[root@mycentos ~]#
[root@mycentos ~]#
[root@mycentos ~]# mkdir /apps
mkdir: cannot create directory '/apps': File exists
[root@mycentos ~]#
[root@mycentos ~]#
[root@mycentos ~]#
[root@mycentos ~]# df -h /apps
Filesystem            Size  Used Avail Use% Mounted on
/dev/mapper/cl-root    50G  3.7G   47G   8% /
[root@mycentos ~]#
[root@mycentos ~]#
[root@mycentos ~]#
```

The command df -h /apps is used to check the location.

In the above screenshot, we can see that the /apps is mounted on the / mount point and /(root) mount point is having 50GB size.

/ mount point is automatically allocated with 50 GB by the linux CentOS operating system as we have selected automatic partitioning while installing CentOS. That is the reason the /apps is also taking the same space from 50GB.

Our goal is to allocate a complete new space to this /apps. Now we will give the command mount /dev/sdb1 /apps. It will mount the new sdb1 disk on /apps.

```
[root@mycentos ~]# mkdir /apps
mkdir: cannot create directory '/apps': File exists
[root@mycentos ~]#
[root@mycentos ~]#
[root@mycentos ~]#
[root@mycentos ~]# df -h /apps
Filesystem            Size  Used Avail Use% Mounted on
/dev/mapper/cl-root    50G  3.7G   47G   8% /
[root@mycentos ~]#
[root@mycentos ~]#
[root@mycentos ~]#
[root@mycentos ~]# mount /dev/sdb1 /apps
[root@mycentos ~]#
[root@mycentos ~]#
[root@mycentos ~]# df -h /apps
Filesystem       Size  Used Avail Use% Mounted on
/dev/sdb1        100G   33M  100G   1% /apps
[root@mycentos ~]#
[root@mycentos ~]#
[root@mycentos ~]#
[root@mycentos ~]#
```

After mounting the sbd1 disk on /apps, we will check whether it is done or not.

We will run the command: df -h /apps.
You can see in the above screenshot that the sdb1 disk is mounted on /apps and /apps will now take 100 GB space from the sdb1 disk.

Now if you save anything in /apps, it will use 100GB space from the sdb1 disk space. The 50 GB root mount point space will not be used.

One issue here is when you restart your system, you again need to manually mount this disk everytime. So to avoid this manual mounting, you need to add this entry to the fstab file.
So give the command: vi /etc/fstab

```
Filesystem            Size  Used Avail Use% Mounted on
/dev/mapper/cl-root    50G  3.7G   47G   8% /
[root@mycentos ~]#
[root@mycentos ~]#
[root@mycentos ~]#
[root@mycentos ~]# mount /dev/sdb1 /apps
[root@mycentos ~]#
[root@mycentos ~]#
[root@mycentos ~]# df -h /apps
Filesystem            Size  Used Avail Use% Mounted on
/dev/sdb1             100G   33M  100G   1% /apps
[root@mycentos ~]#
[root@mycentos ~]#
[root@mycentos ~]#
[root@mycentos ~]# vi /etc/fstab
```

The screen will now look like below and you need to go to the last entry line or end of the file.

```
                              root@mycentos:~
 File  Edit  View  Search  Terminal  Help

#
# /etc/fstab
# Created by anaconda on Wed Nov  8 05:29:11 2017
#
# Accessible filesystems, by reference, are maintained under '/dev/disk'
# See man pages fstab(5), findfs(8), mount(8) and/or blkid(8) for more info
#
/dev/mapper/cl-root      /                       xfs     defaults        0 0
UUID=08def03a-39ac-425a-9bed-688f84f2f792 /boot   xfs     defaults        0 0
/dev/mapper/cl-home      /home                   xfs     defaults        0 0
/dev/mapper/cl-swap      swap                    swap    defaults        0 0
```

First give the disk name as /dev/sdb1. Then give the directory name on which it is mounted as /apps. Give the file system type as xfs.

```
                                        root@mycentos:~

  File  Edit  View  Search  Terminal  Help

#
# /etc/fstab
# Created by anaconda on Wed Nov  8 05:29:11 2017
#
# Accessible filesystems, by reference, are maintained under '/dev/disk'
# See man pages fstab(5), findfs(8), mount(8) and/or blkid(8) for more info
#
/dev/mapper/cl-root         /                     xfs     defaults        0 0
UUID=08def03a-39ac-425a-9bed-686f84f2f792 /boot              xfs      defaults        0 0
/dev/mapper/cl-home         /home         xfs     defaults        0 0
/dev/mapper/cl-swap         swap          swap    defaults        0 0
/dev/sdb1                   /apps         xfs     defaults        0 0
```

Then save the entry by w command.

This is the way we add a new hard disk to the Linux server.

First we need to add the hard disk at the VM level. Then within the server, we need to format the disk and mount it on a directory.

Add new network card to VM

In this lesson, we will learn about adding a new network card into the virtual machine.

There might be a requirement that you need two interfaces, two network cards or two network interfaces in your virtual machine. We can take the example of Oracle RAC where you have multiple networks (one can be a public network and one could be private network). Here you communicate to the VM via two different networks. By default, one network card is allocated when you create a virtual machine. But you can add more network cards.

Here we will learn how to add a new network card, how to assign a new IP address to this new network card and how it works.

We will go the settings of the virtual machine My_cent_OS and go to the network option.

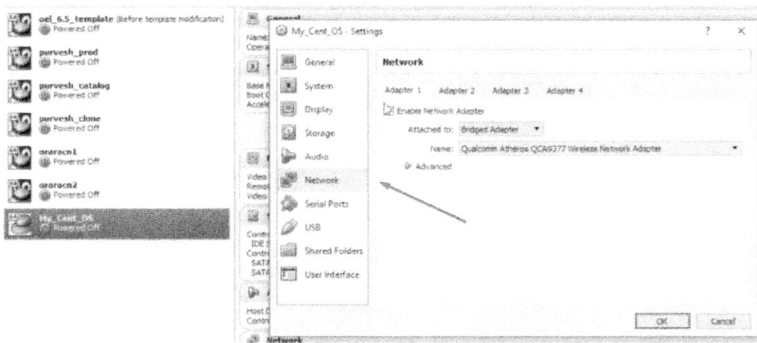

In the above screenshot, we can see that the Adapter 1 is the default network card which is allocated and is in the Bridged Adapter mode.

A virtualbox allows you to add a maximum of 4 network cards but that situation comes very rarely.

Go to the Adapter 2 and enable the Network Adapter and make sure the adapter is in Bridged Adapter mode.

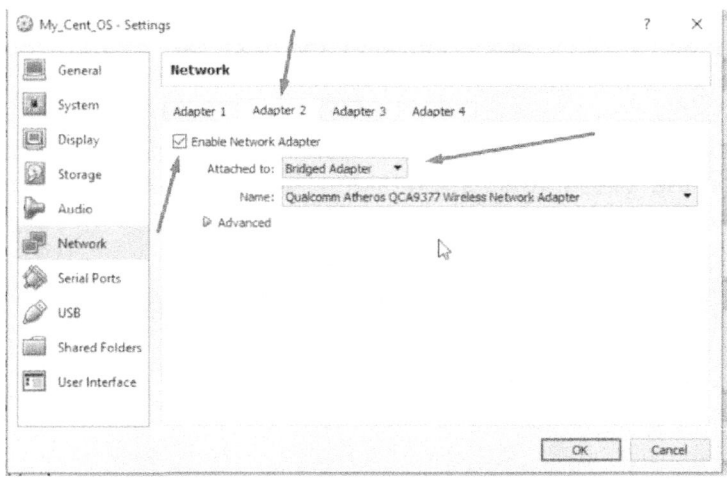

Then go to the **Advanced** button and you will get the MAC address. Copy the MAC address. You need to give the MAC address in the virtual machine once you start the operating system.

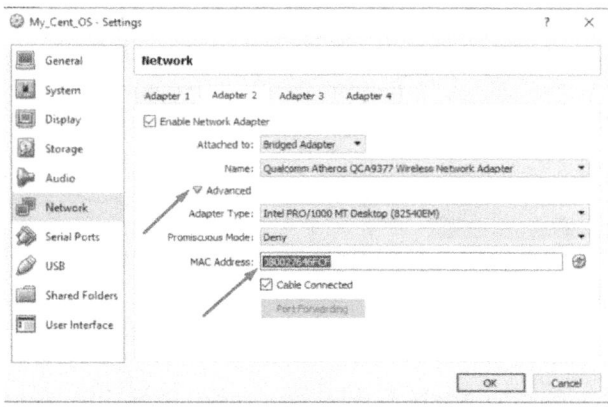

So copy the MAC address and keep it handy and then start the Virtual machine.

Before going further, we will define the steps to add a network card:

1. Add the network card at VM level.
2. Copy the MAC address.
3. Add new network interface in CentOS.

So we already are done with the first two steps. Now we will proceed for the 3rd step.

Here we actually have to add a new network interface in the server. So, on the Virtual machine desktop, we will click on the small arrow icon on the corner.

When you click on the icon, you will see the network interfaces

126

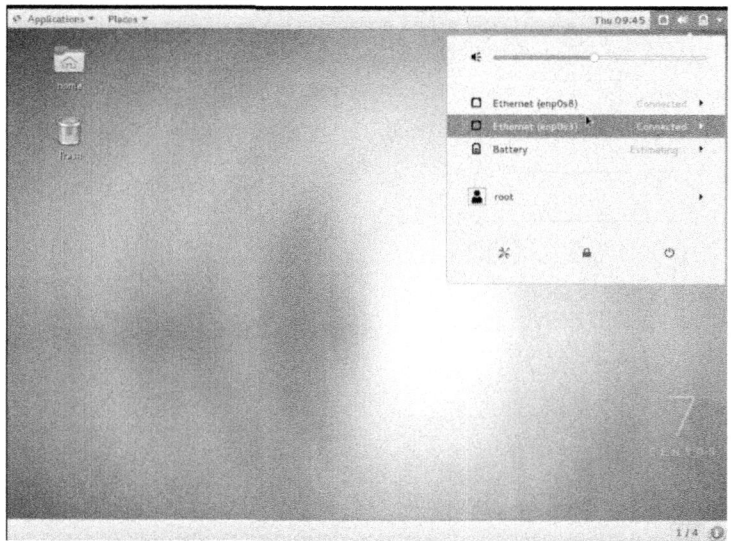

We have two interfaces there. We have already created one interface in the previous lessons.

When you click on the Wired settings of the second one, you will see that the IP address is already allocated automatically dynamically to the network card.

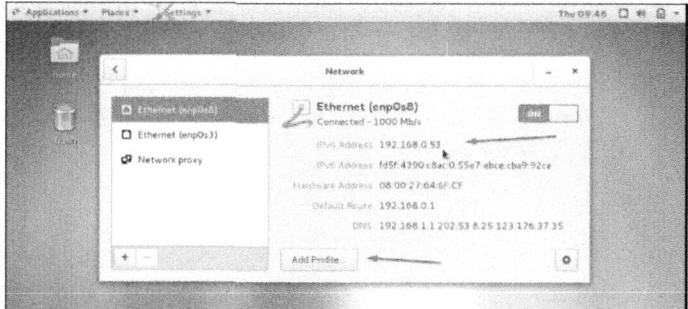

So the IP address is automatically allocated in this CentOS 7 version. You do not have to add it. You need to do it in the earlier versions CentOS 5 or 6.

Let us suppose that you want to change the IP address. You need to click on the Gear icon.

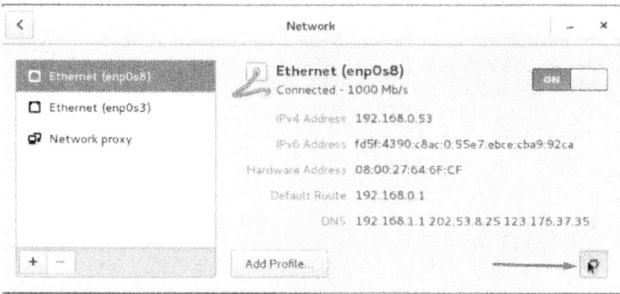

The screen will come like the below screen.

Go the IPv4 option and choose "Manual" option under Addresses.

Then depending upon the IP address choice you got from your IT team, you can feed into the network.

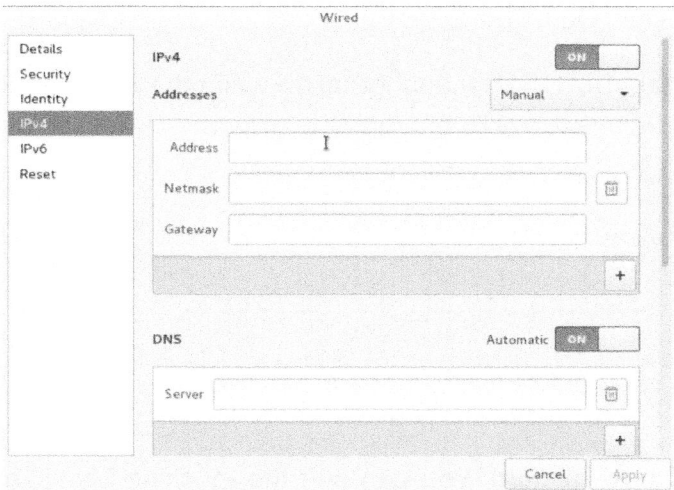

So this is how you add a network card to the virtual machine. First you will add a network interface at the VM level. Then you add the network card interface in the OS but with CentOS 7, you don't need to add it. It will pick it up automatically.

Taking virtual machine snapshots

In this lesson, we will discuss about a very important feature called **Snapshots**.

Suppose you want to test something on a virtual machine but you do not know whether the test will give you a positive result or not. You can actually save the state of the virtual machine and then you perform the test. In case the test goes wrong, you can come back to the saved state of the virtual machine.

So this helps you perform all the testing that you want to perform on any virtual machine. If the testing shows negative results, you can always roll back to the original state of the virtual machine.

The saved state explained in the above paragraph is known as Snapshots.

There are two types of Snapshots:

1. Hot Snapshot

2. Cold Snapshot

Hot Snapshot: The snapshot taken while the virtual machine is up and running.

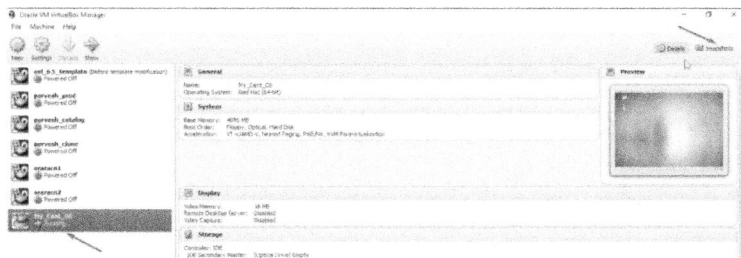

In the above picture, you can see the machine My_Cent_OS is up and running. We will click on the Snapshot button on the right up corner.

Then click on the button as shown in the below picture to take a snapshot of the virtual machine.

Another window will open to take the snapshot.

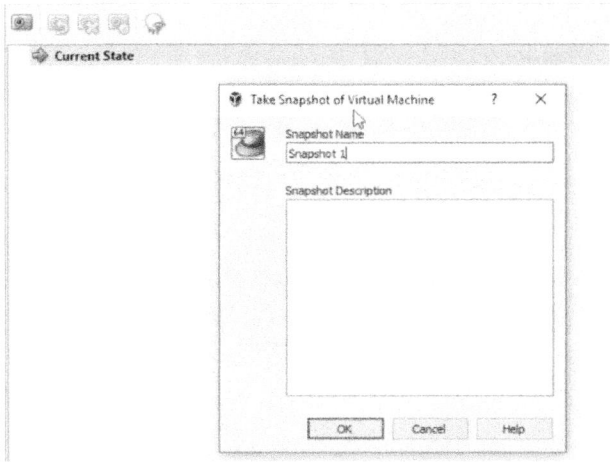

We will take a snapshot. Then we will create a new user and then we will try to roll back.

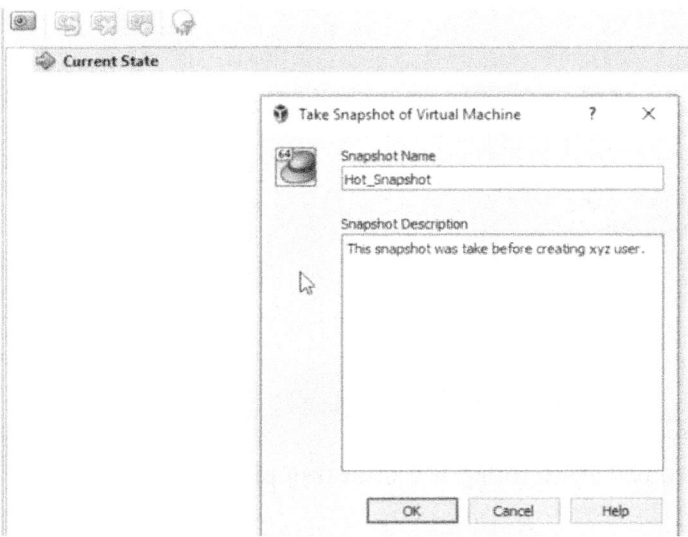

The above picture shows that we are taking a snapshot of the VM when it is up and running before creating a new user.

Once you click on OK button, it will show that it is taking the snapshot.

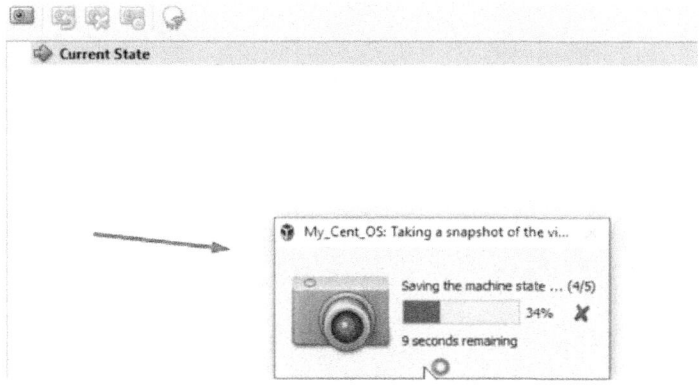

When the snapshot is taken, you will see that the snapshot is taken with the current time mentioned.

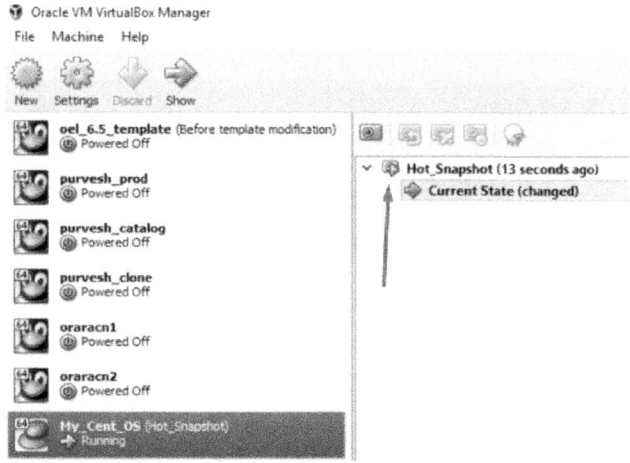

Now we will try to make the changes in VM.

Open a new terminal inside the virtual machine

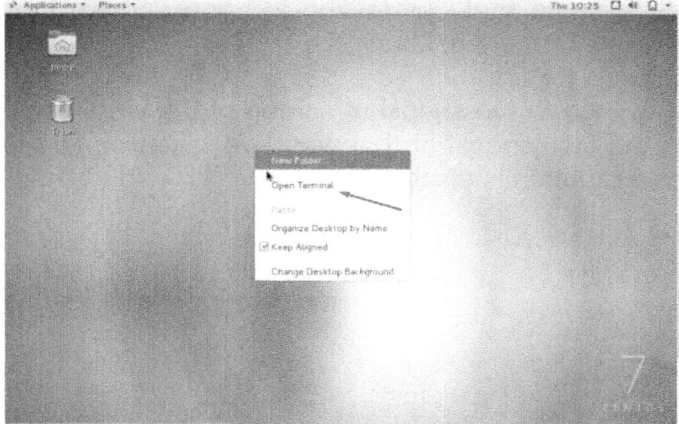

When you click on Open terminal, it will show as

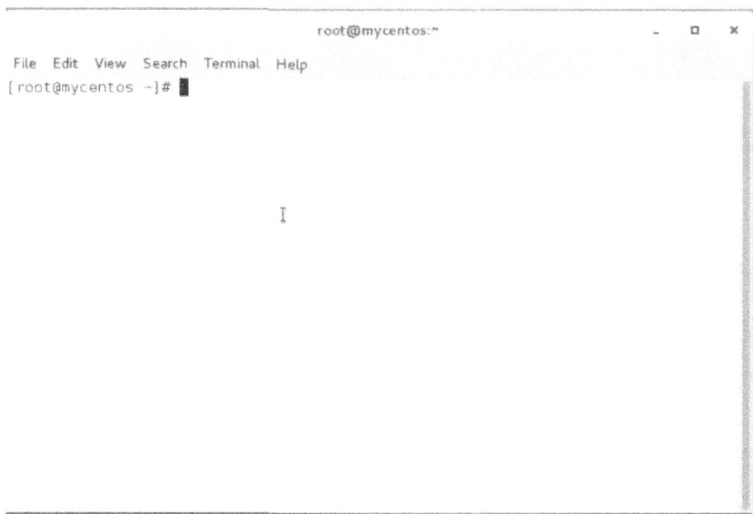

We will add a new user xyz.

Now we assume that our testing is done and we have negative results. So we want to roll back.

Now we will go to the snapshot screen of the virtual machine. Right click on the Hot_snapshot that we have taken earlier. You will see that Restore button is disabled.

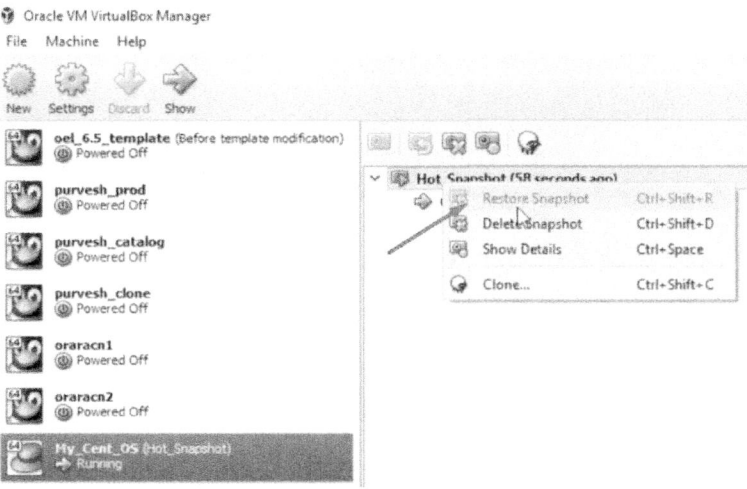

The restore button is disabled as the VM is up and running. So, you need to shut down or power off the VM to restore the VM terminal.

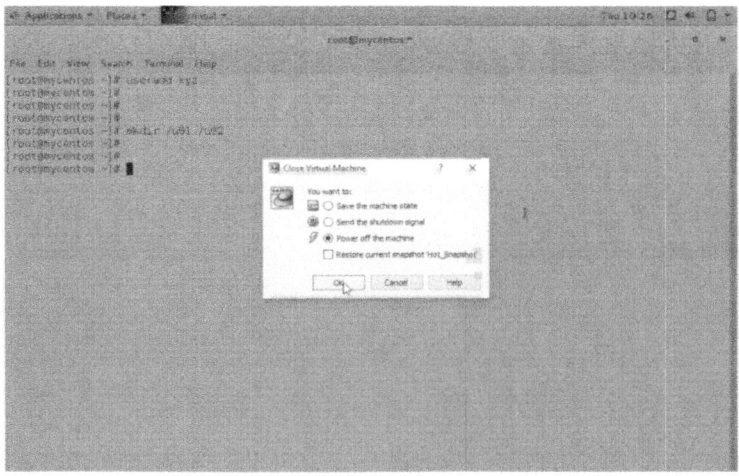

Now you can check that the restore button is enabled.

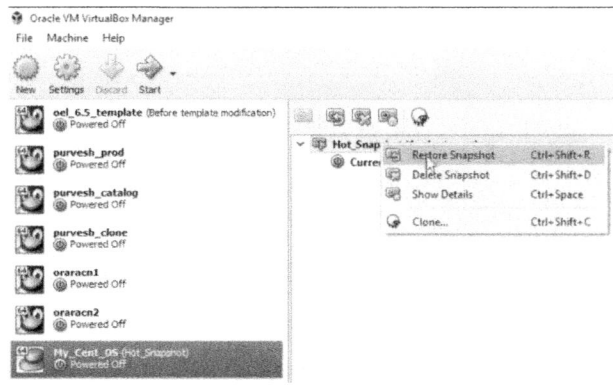

You can even select the restore option here as shown below.

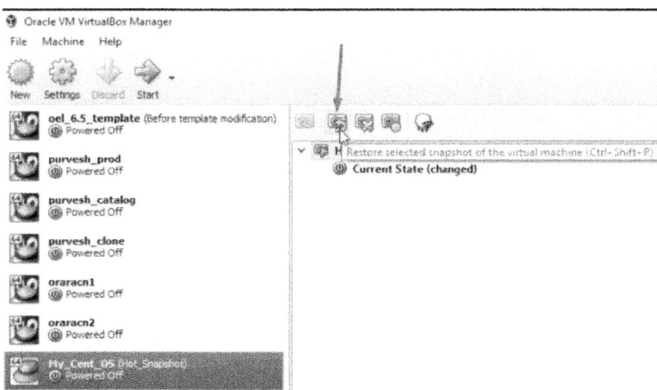

When you click on Restore button, a window will open asking you if you really want to roll back or restore.

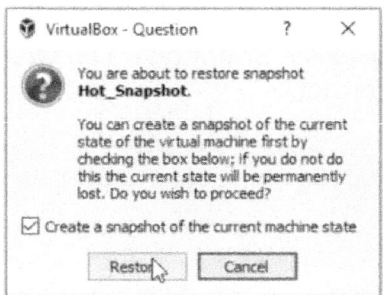

It will also ask you to create a current machine state snapshot. So we will restore the previous state with creating a current snapshot.

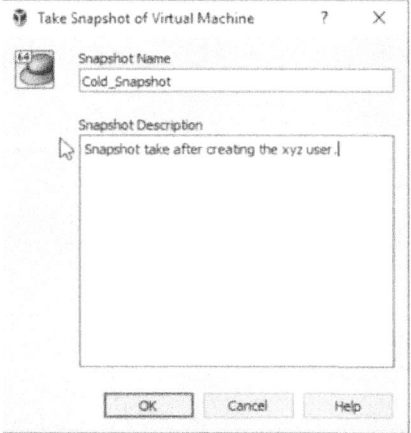

Click on Ok and the VM is restored to the previous state.

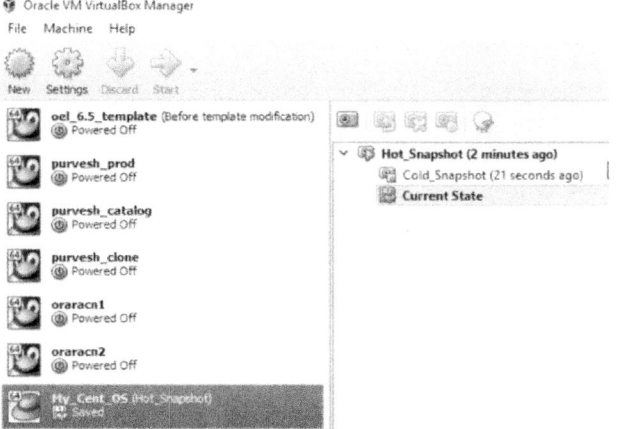

Now we will start the VM and verify whether the new user that we have created (xyz) exists or not and also whether the directory u01 and u02 are there or not.

We can see that the xyz user does not exist and the directories u01 and u02 are also not there.

So the snapshot process is very simple. Before testing anything on VM, you need to take a snapshot and then do the testing. If you are not satisfied with the results, you can always rollback. You can also prefer to take a snapshot of the VM state after the testing is done so that whenever you want, you can again go to some further testing.

Now I will power off the terminal or the virtual machine and I want to again go back to the cold snapshot (the VM state after testing) where we have the xyz user and u01 and u02 directories.

So we will start the VM again with root user login. Then we will open a terminal.

Then go for the commands: id xyz and ls -ld /u01 /u02

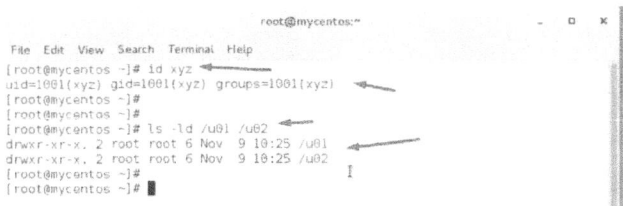

We can see that the user xyz is there and also the directories u01 and u02 are also there in the system.

So we can save the snapshots of the Virtual machine at different states and we can rollback at any state to perform the respective activities.

Create virtual machine clone

In this lesson, we will learn about VM clone.

Suppose you want to practice something on the virtual machine and you want to have another machine where you want to install CentOS. Practically, you will think about creating another virtual machine and install CentOS on that. But you can also clone an existing machine in virtualbox and then you can use that clone machine as another VM.

We will go through the steps of making a clone of an existing VM now.

Right click on the VM and click on the clone option

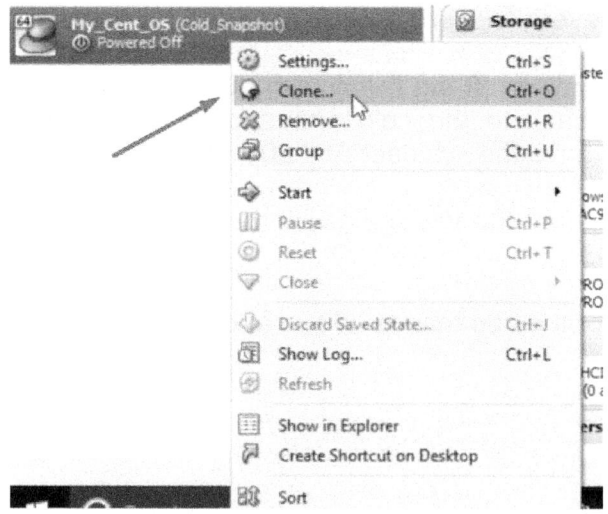

It will open a window and ask to enter a name to the clone of that VM. Give a name to the clone.

Also you need to enable the option for Reinitialize the MAC address of all network cards. You need to enable this as two machines cannot have the same MAC address. So the VM will allocate new

MAC address to the network cards of the new machine. Otherwise if you do not enable this option, you will not be able to run the two machines at the same time as the two MAC address will collide.

Then click on Next

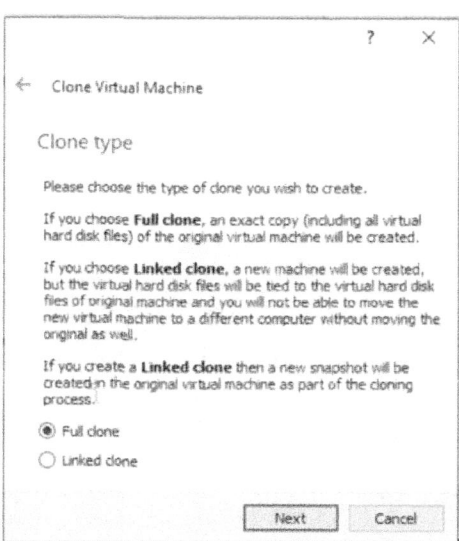

You will get the option to choose between Full clone and a Linked clone. A linked clone will be linked to the original VM machine which we will not prefer. A full clone is an independent clone where whatever you do will not impact the parent or the original machine.

So go with the Full clone option and click on Next.

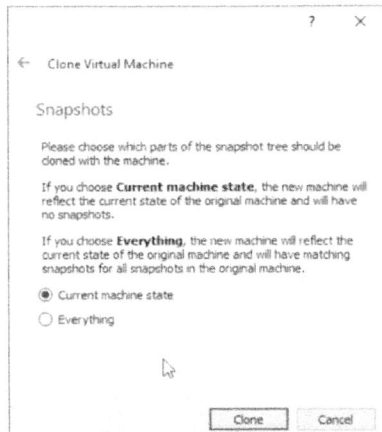

We will get the option to choose from Current machine state or Everything. When you choose Everything, you will get all the snapshots also in the clone whereas you will get the clone of the current state of the original machine when you choose Current machine state.

We will choose the current machine state. Then click on Clone.

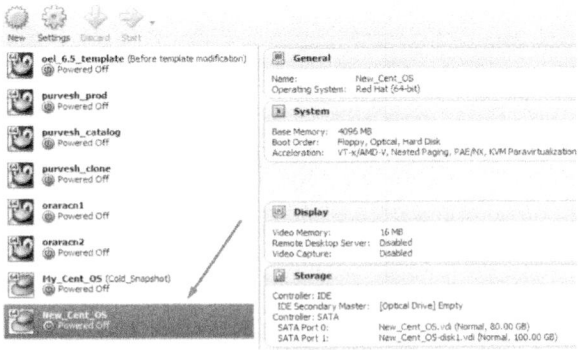

You will get a new CentOS machine within minutes. You don't really need to create a new virtual machine. You don't have to install the CentOS. You do not have to install the apps that you might be working again on to the new system. You do not have to fix the network.

Also you can create any number of clones until the system memory will support. You need to be careful on the collective size of RAM of all the VMs that are running. It should not exceed the RAM of the host system. Also you need to have a separate 4GB of RAM dedicated to your host system.

There are some post VM clone activities which you must perform immediately after you create a clone.

- Change the hostname. Once you clone, the host names will remain the same. So you need to change the name of the created clone.
- Change the IP address. You need to change the IP address of the clone as it will collide with the IP of the original machine.

You can start the clone virtual machine and check for the xyz user and u01 and u02 directories in it.

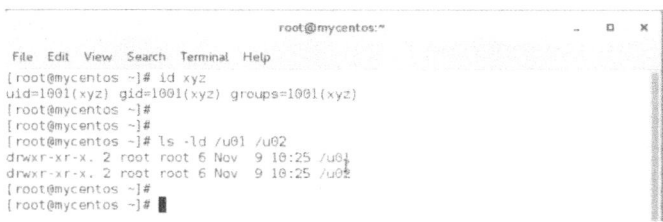

So, your clone machine is the exact replica of your original virtual machine and it is very easy and simple to create a clone.

Saving virtual machine state

In this lesson, we will learn about saving the virtual machine state.

Suppose you want to shut down the virtual machine and you want the virtual machine to start again (whenever you start) from the point where you have stopped it.

Suppose I am working on VM and I want to shut down my windows system (host system). So rather that shutting down the VM or doing the Power off of the VM, I will save the state of the VM.

So I will directly click on the cross button of the machine or the close button of the machine.

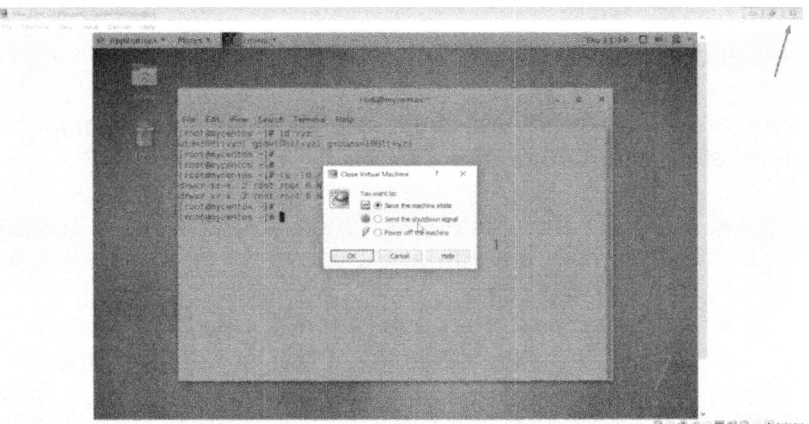

When you directly close the VM, it will ask you to choose from the 3 options:

- Save the machine state
- Send the shutdown signal
- Power off the machine

We will have a closer look at the options

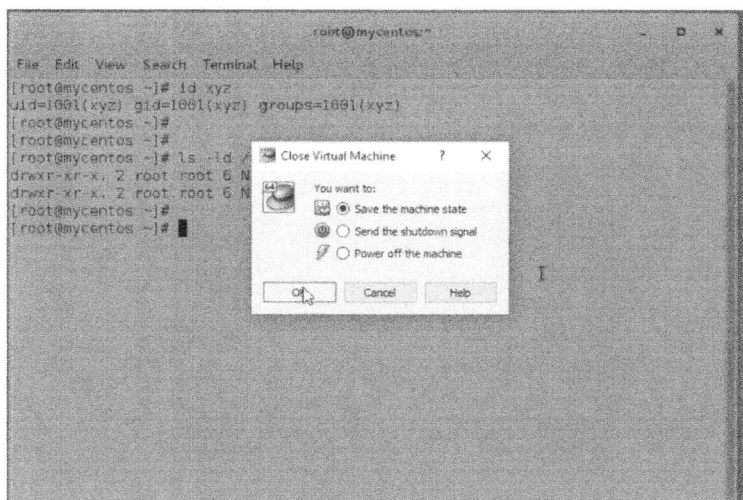

We will choose the option as "Save the machine state". It will save the virtual machine in the same state or point where you stopped working.

You can see the machine New_Cent_OS is in Saved mode.

Now when you start the same machine, it will start from the same place where you stopped it.

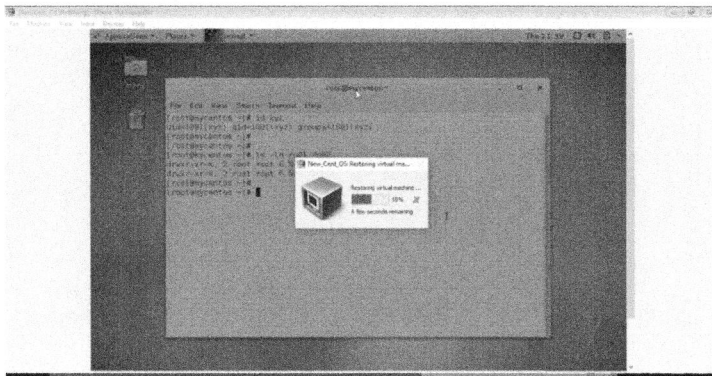

So, it is an important feature where you don't have to worry about saving your work inside the VM if you want to shut down your PC or laptop or the host (windows) machine. You just have to save the machine state and whenever you start it again, you can start from the same point where you were while shutting your system off.

Export and Import appliances

In this lesson, we will learn about sharing the virtual machine with other users.

Suppose you want to share the virtual machine on which you are practicing with your friends. You can share the virtual machine in an open virtualization archive (OVA) format.

You can create one single file on your operating system and later you can share that file with your friends. They can import that file into their virtualbox or VMware. So this is a way to clone the VMs on different servers. We will learn this using export and import methods.

Go to File and click on Export Appliance

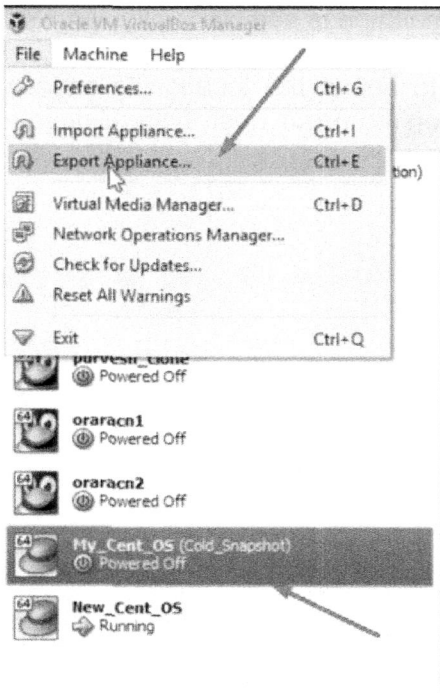

You will get a window for Export Virtual Appliance

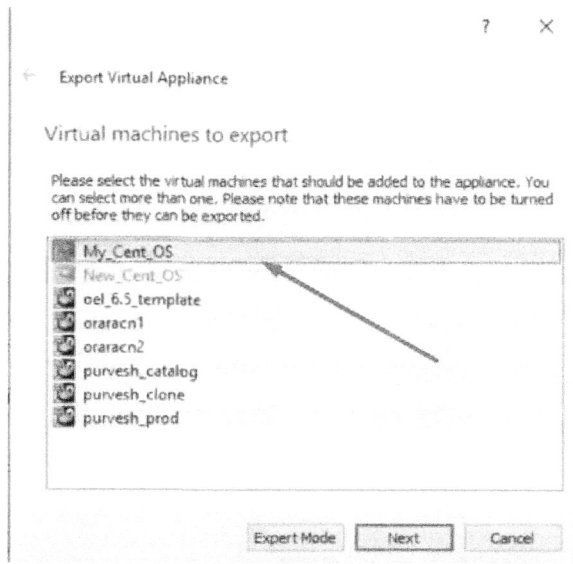

Make sure the machine is selected. Click on Next

It will ask you to select the location to save the .ova file. We will choose a location from our host system drive. Keep the format as OVF 1.0.

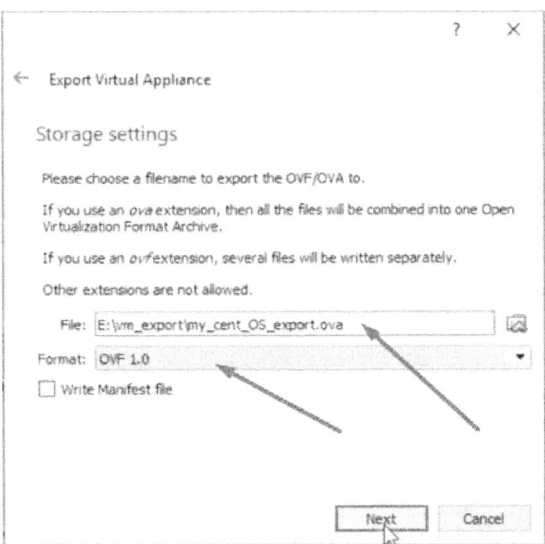

Click on Next

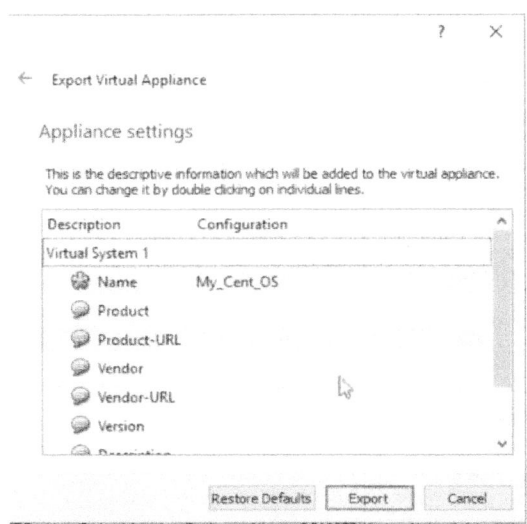

You can give the product, product URL, vendor, vendor-URL,version and more in the settings.

Then we will choose the Export button directly.

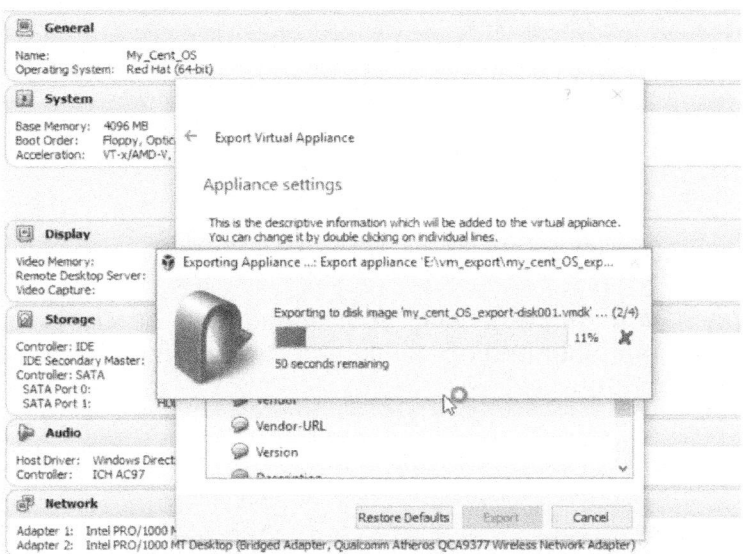

It will start creating an open virtualization file (one single file of the entire virtual machine). You can use this file to share among your friends. They can import this file to any virtualization platform (VMware, EXSI etc) as the extension of the file is .ova which means the file is not dependent on any virtualization platform. It can be read by all the virtualization platforms.

Let us take an example to this export and import feature. Suppose a person is having some multiple servers. One can create VM templates. One can install windows in one virtual machine and consider it as windows template. Now one can export the machine and keep the file. Similarly one can install REDHAT on one VM and can export the machine and keep the file. Now if a person wants to deploy a windows machine, he will not create a VM and install windows. He will actually import the template and simply use it.

Suppose you install all the packages required in the template file or the template virtual machine. Use the export feature. When you will import the template, you will get all the packages pre-installed in it.

You don't have to again install those packages.

Now after the file gets saved, it will look like below.

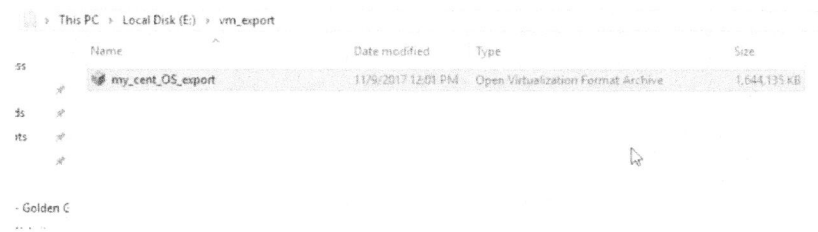

You can see that the file is in OVA or OVF format.

Suppose you share it with your friend. He needs to go to the virtualbox manager and open File and click on Import Appliance.

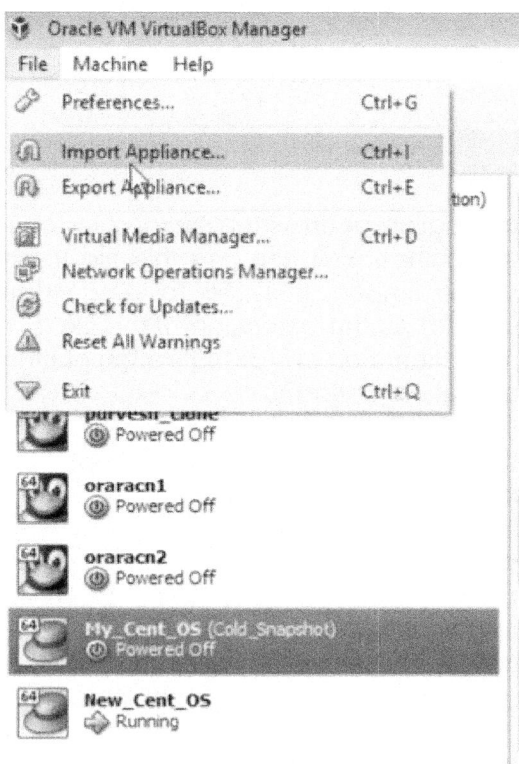

It will ask the location of the file from your local folder.

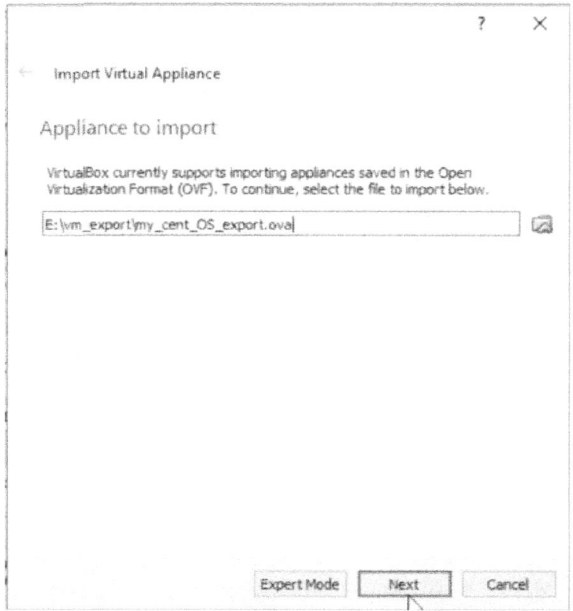

After selecting the file path, click on Next.

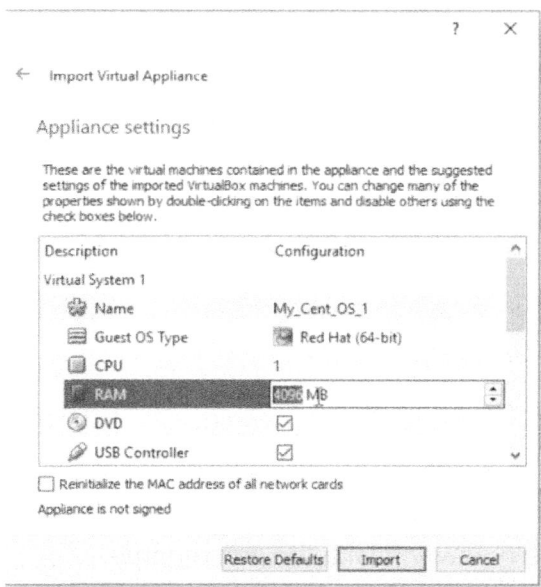

It will show you the details of the file. You can decrease the RAM as per your requirement. If you are importing the virtual machine in the same environment (in the same organization), make sure to reinitialize the MAC address. If you are giving it to your friend or someone who is in a different location, then you do not have to do this.

The concept is the parent machine (original VM) and the clone VM are in the same network, then you need to reinitialize the MAC address so that it will not collide. If they are on different networks, you do not have to do this.

In my case, the two machines are on the same network. So I will tick mark that option.

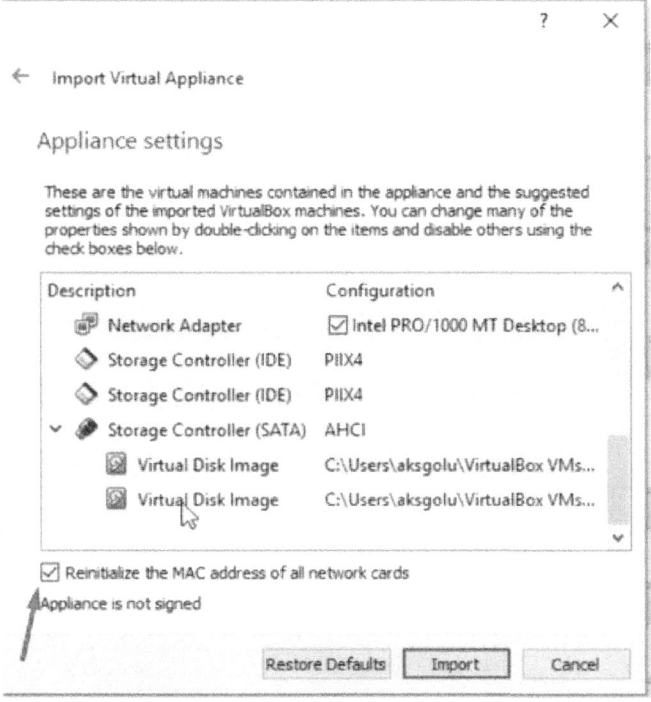

Then click on Import.

You will have a new VM with the same name.

So there are two ways of cloning:

1. Right click and choose clone.

2. Use Export Appliance on the VM and save the file in OVA format and share. Then use Import Appliance to import the virtual machine.

## CHAPTER 6

Must know DBA Tools

Introduction to Putty

Once the Linux installation is done, we need to understand that the real time setup is different that our practice setup.

In real time, the Linux server are placed at different locations. We, as DBA, do not get option to physically login to the server and work.

In real time, every organization or the DBAs or even the system administrators use a tool called as PuTTY to remotely login on the Linux server.

In the same way as we have a linux server installed on the virtual machine, we need not work directly on the virtual machine. We will also use the PuTTY tool in order to connect to the virtual machine.

So let us go ahead and download the PuTTY software.

Open the web browser and search for PuTTY. Click on the first option.

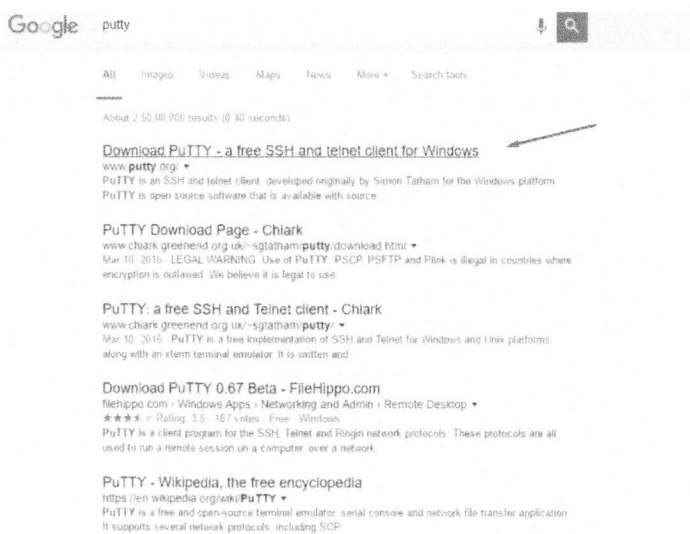

You will get the option to download PuTTY

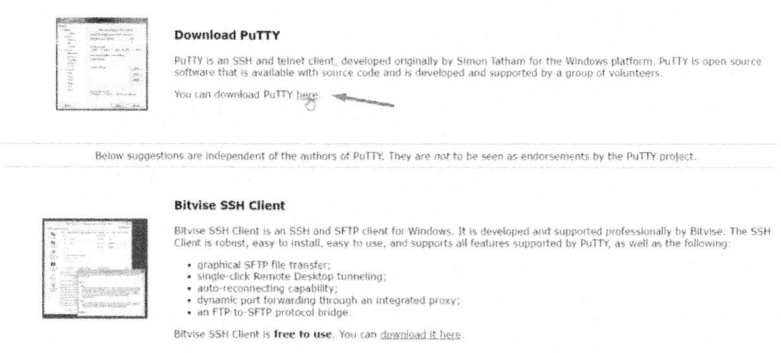

Click on the link and you will get another page for PuTTY links.

Remember that PuTTY is a very small software. You don't have to install the software really. Just download and use it.

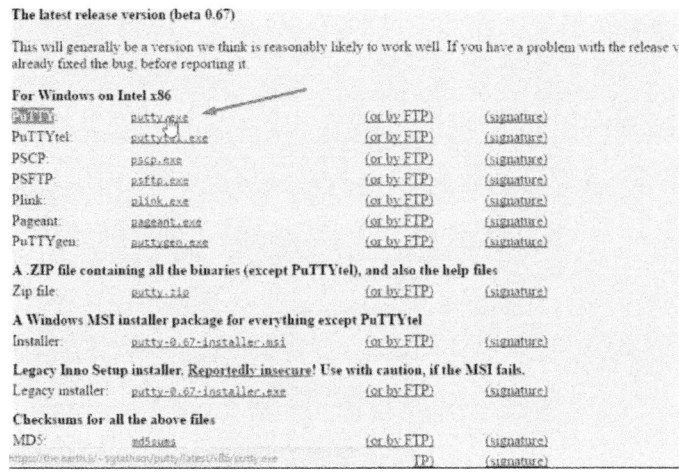

The latest release version (beta 0.67)

This will generally be a version we think is reasonably likely to work well. If you have a problem with the release v already fixed the bug, before reporting it

For Windows on Intel x86

PuTTY:	putty.exe	(or by FTP)	(signature)
PuTTYtel:	puttytel.exe	(or by FTP)	(signature)
PSCP:	pscp.exe	(or by FTP)	(signature)
PSFTP:	psftp.exe	(or by FTP)	(signature)
Plink:	plink.exe	(or by FTP)	(signature)
Pageant:	pageant.exe	(or by FTP)	(signature)
PuTTYgen:	puttygen.exe	(or by FTP)	(signature)

A .ZIP file containing all the binaries (except PuTTYtel), and also the help files

| Zip file: | putty.zip | (or by FTP) | (signature) |

A Windows MSI installer package for everything except PuTTYtel

| Installer: | putty-0.67-installer.msi | (or by FTP) | (signature) |

Legacy Inno Setup installer. Reportedly insecure! Use with caution, if the MSI fails.

| Legacy installer: | putty-0.67-installer.exe | (or by FTP) | (signature) |

Checksums for all the above files

| MD5: | md5sums | (or by FTP) | (signature) |

https://the.earth.li/~sgtatham/putty/latest/x86/putty.exe   (P)   (signature)

Click on the default first link.

Once the download is completed, start the PuTTY tool.

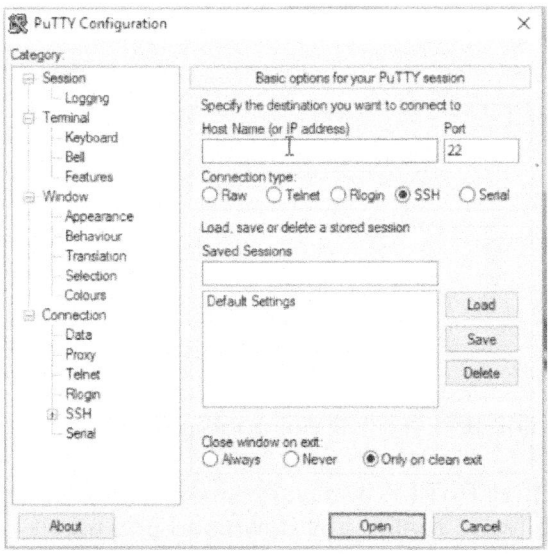

In the Host Name field, we need to give the host name or the IP address of the linux server where we would like to connect. The default port number for connecting Linux servers is 22 for the SSH connections. The connection type in PuTTY is SSH (default).

We will give one host name or the IP address and try to connect to a server.

Click on Open and it will connect to the server with IP as 192.168.0.200

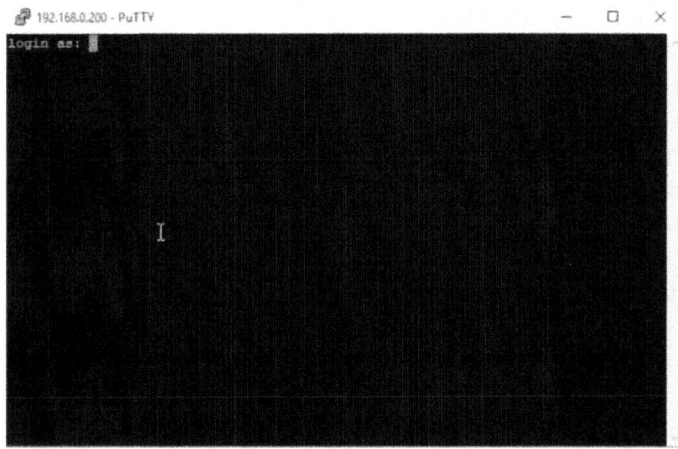

Now we are connected to our Linux server.

We will login as root user and give the root user password. Then hit Enter. We will connect to the OEL 5 installation that we have already done.

We will check by typing hostname and it will show oel5.oraclegenesis.com. This is the host name that we gave while installing the Linux on virtual machine.

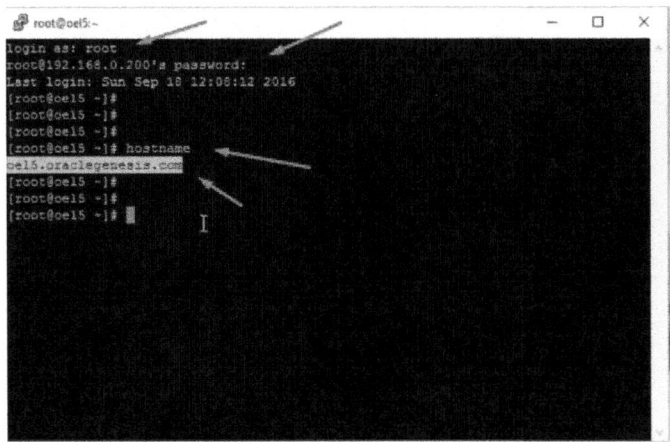

It is a very small tool but it has lots of settings. We will look into some of the settings of PuTTY which you might need in future to setup your PuTTY interface.

Right click on the title bar.

Do not right click inside PuTTY. If you right click inside, it will paste the data from the clipboard. Suppose you have highlighted something inside PuTTY and then you do the right click inside the interface. Highlighting anything will copy that thing and right clicking will paste that thing.

After right clicking on the title bar, go to change settings

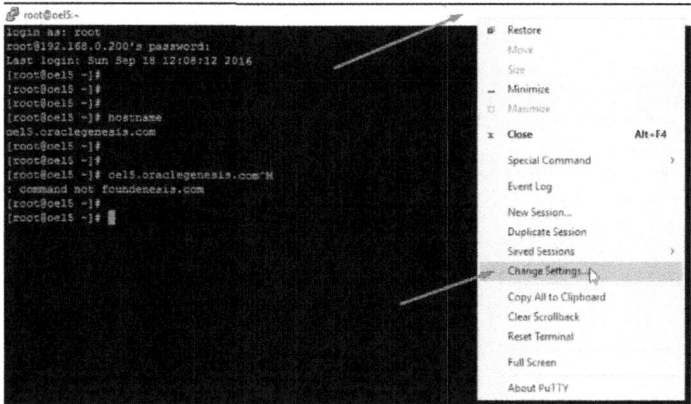

Remember the settings we are getting into now will impact the current session or the current PuTTY which is open.

First we will go to Appearance tab in the settings window

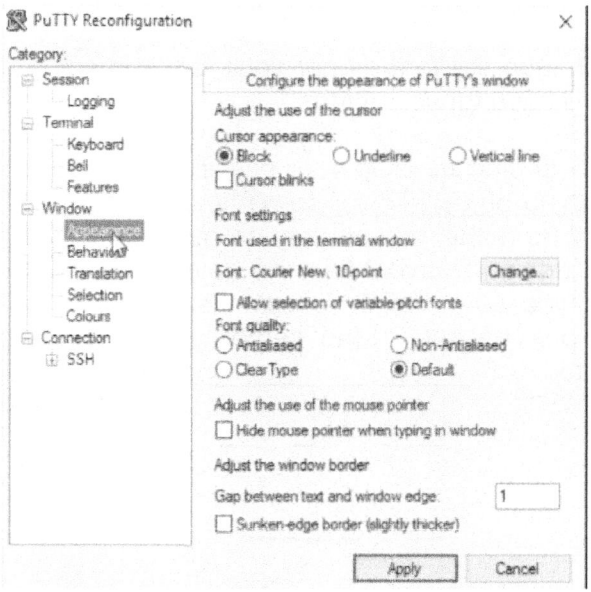

We have font settings where we can change the font size, font style and font type.

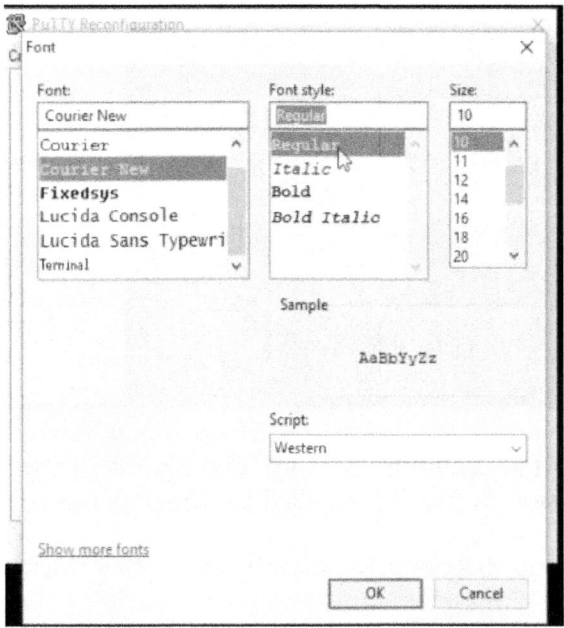

You can change the font as per your requirement or liking and your terminal will have those settings.

We have a setting to keep your session alive. Suppose we are not doing anything on PuTTY for some time(say a minute or less). It will disconnect from the server very frequently and yo need to login again and again. To avoid this, we have a keep alive setting where you can guide your PuTTY session such that it will automatically send a blank packet to the server and the session will not be disconnected.

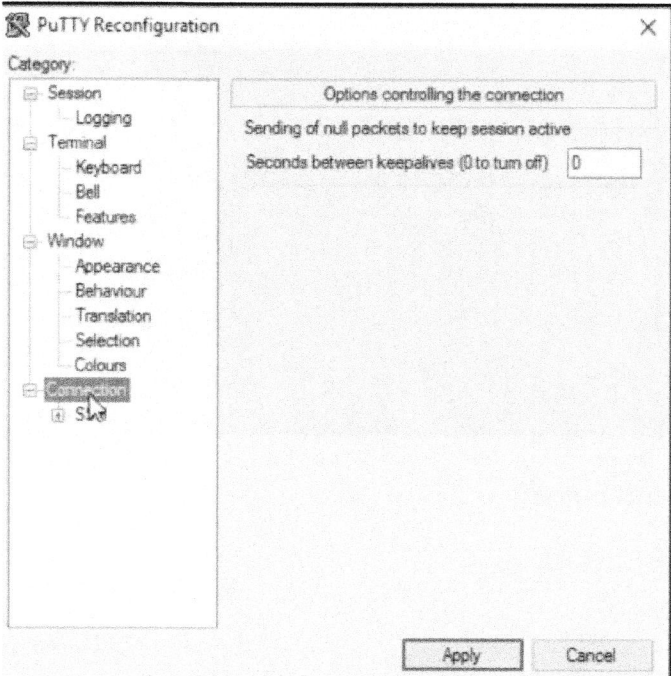

You can put anything above 3 to 10 (recommended). Then click on Apply and the session will continue even when you are on a break.

Now suppose you want to Save a PuTTY session or the settings which you have set for your session so that you don't have to change the settings again and again whenever you login.

Right click on the title bar of the terminal and go to change settings

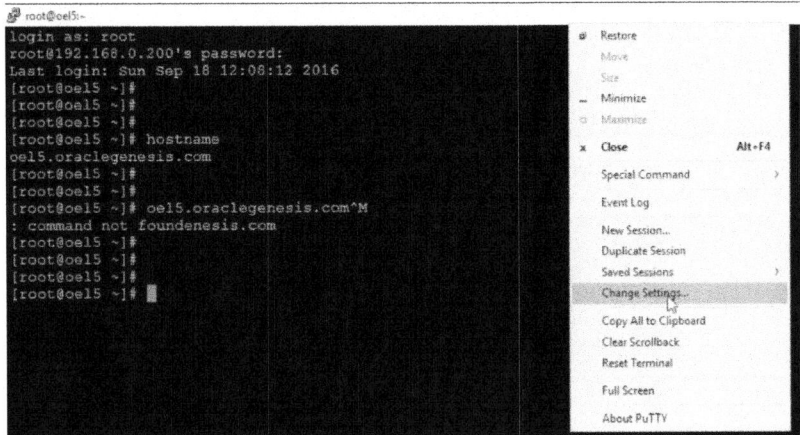

Then go to Session

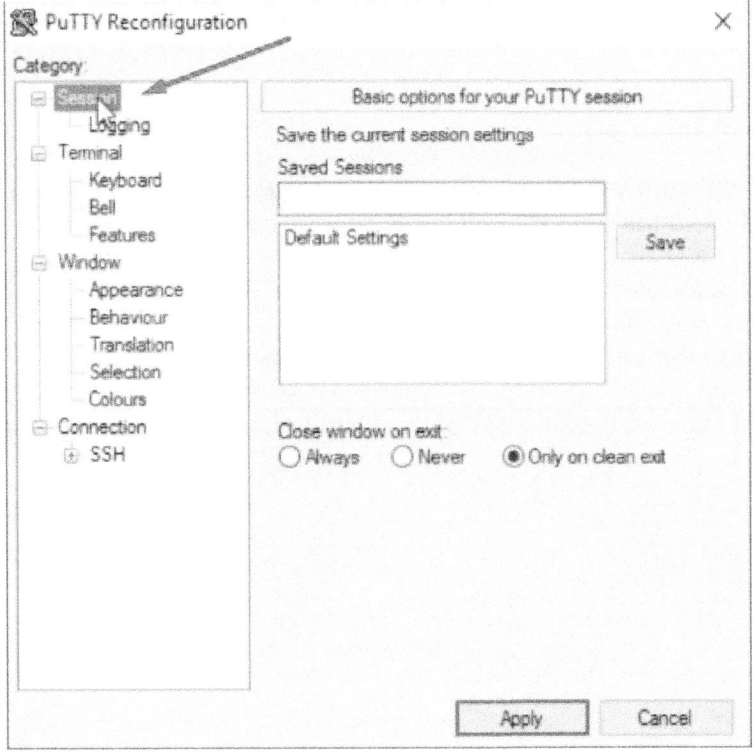

Then give a name to the session (say oel5)

Then click on Save. The entire session details will be saved in oel5. Then click on Apply.

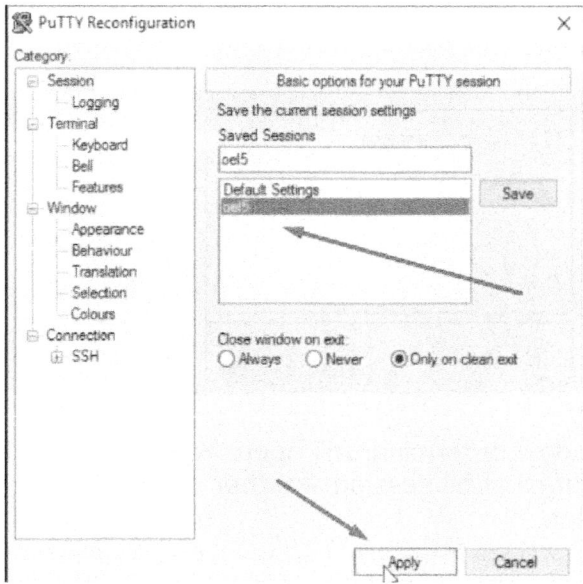

Now we will try to open a new session.

Right click on the title bar and go to New Session

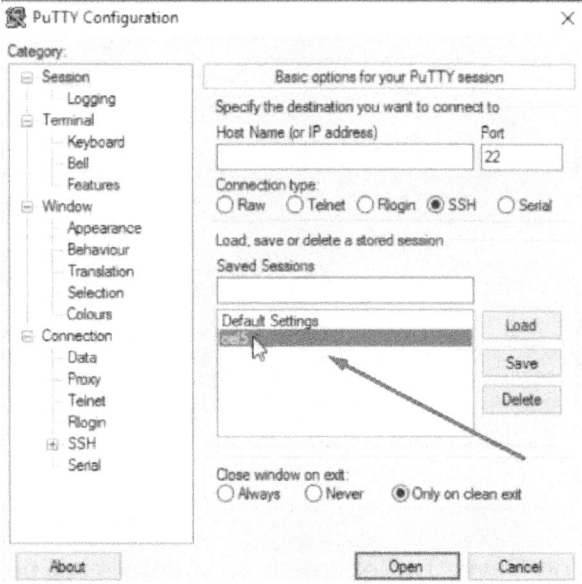

You can see oel5 in the saved sessions. Highlight it and click on Open.

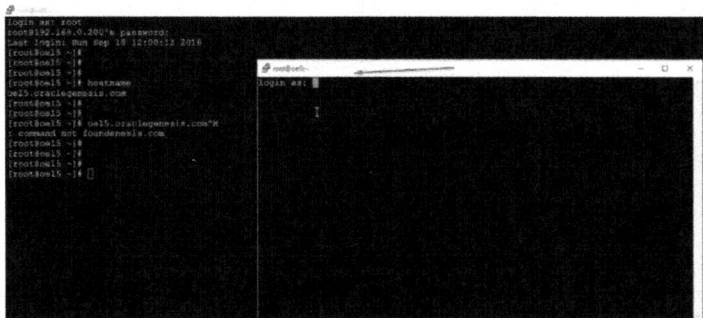

A new window or terminal will open. You can check the settings for this new terminal or session whether it is the same which we have saved or not.

Now suppose you want to debug the connection between PuTTY and Linux server.

Right click on the title bar of the PuTTY session and go to the Event log option

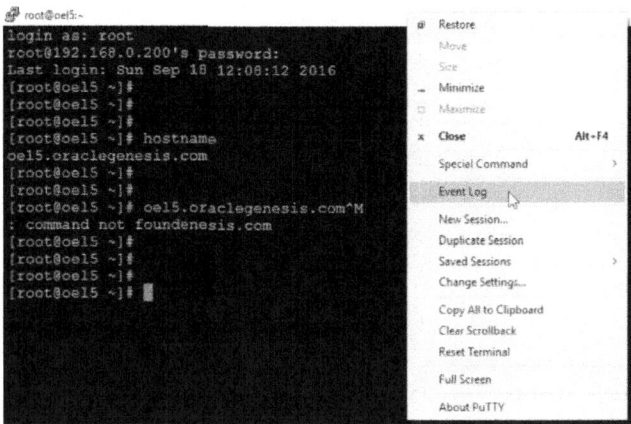

A window will open up showing all the events that happened in order to connect to the target server.

Suppose your PuTTY is not able to connect to the server. You can go to the event log and check where it is going wrong or you can use these logs to talk to your network team.

These were some features about PuTTY.

Introduction to WinSCP

In the previous lessons, we have learnt how to install linux on virtual machine and also how to use PuTTY to connect to a server.

Sometimes you might have to copy file from your windows machine to the linux server. PuTTY does not give you any such interface. Suppose you have downloaded any software on your windows machine. Now you want to copy that software from your windows machine to the linux server. We can use a tool called WinSCP to do this.

Let us first download the tool WinSCP.

Click on the first result. Then a screen will open.

You need to click on the Installation package.

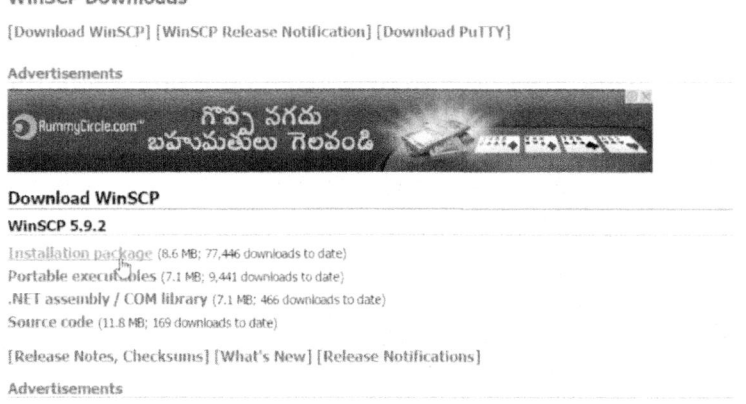

The download will start. Once the download is complete, we need to install it.

First accept the license agreement

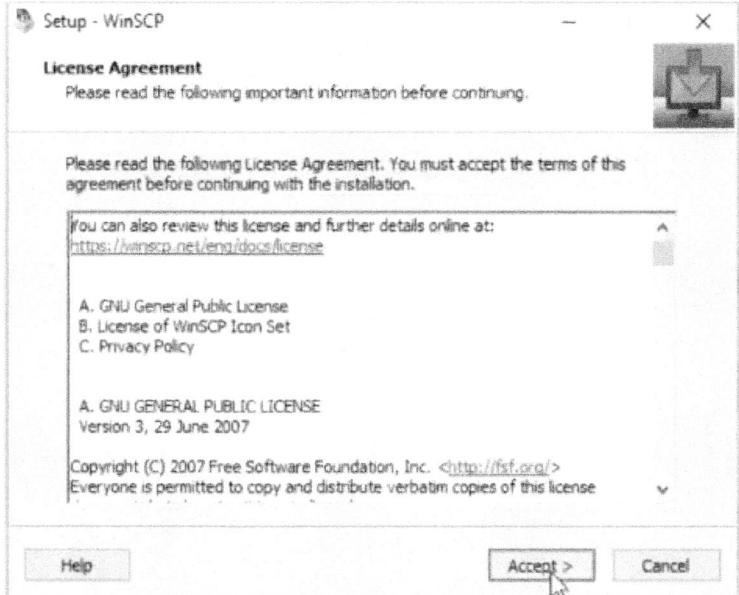

Then in the next two screens, just click on Next and then install.

Now this will prompt you for importing the saved sessions in your PuTTY to WinSCP.

Choose Yes.

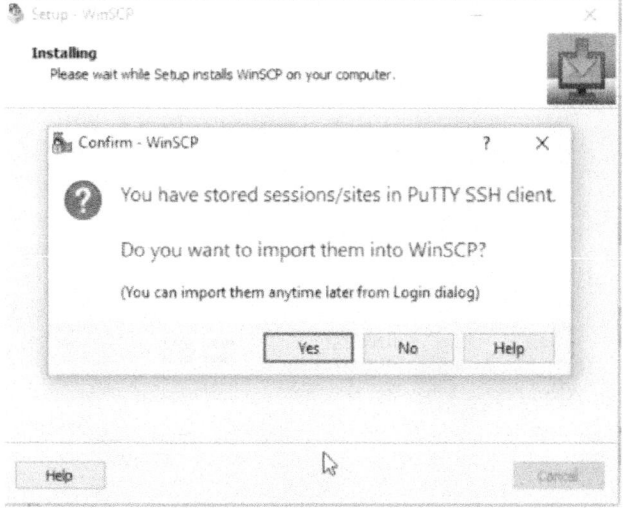

Then click on Ok

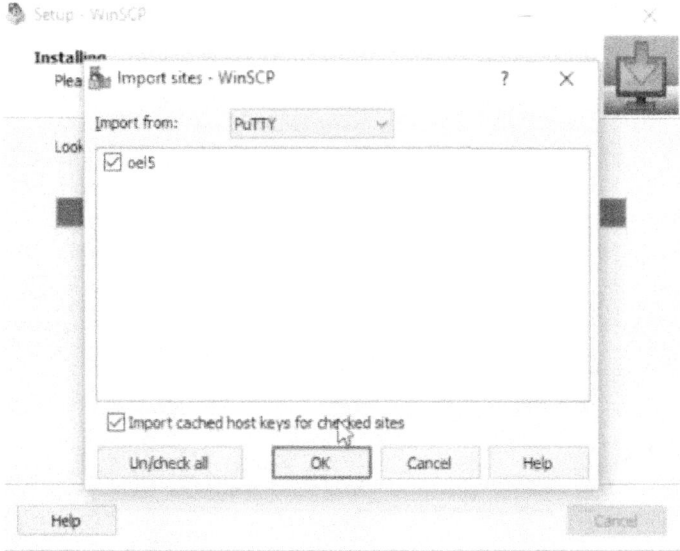

Then click on Finish

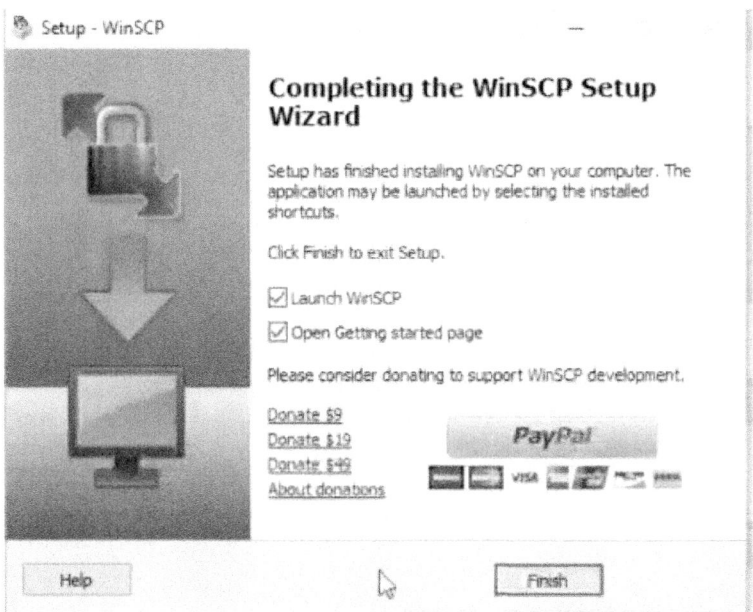

Now the WinSCP window will open

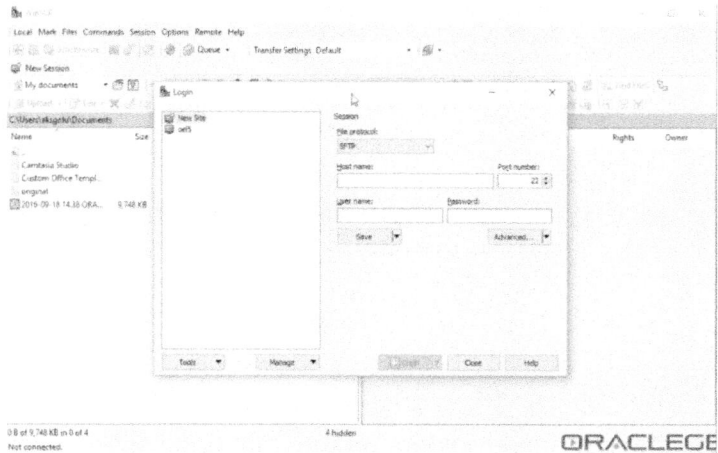

You can connect to the linux server in the same way as you connect through PuTTY to Linux server by providing the IP address.

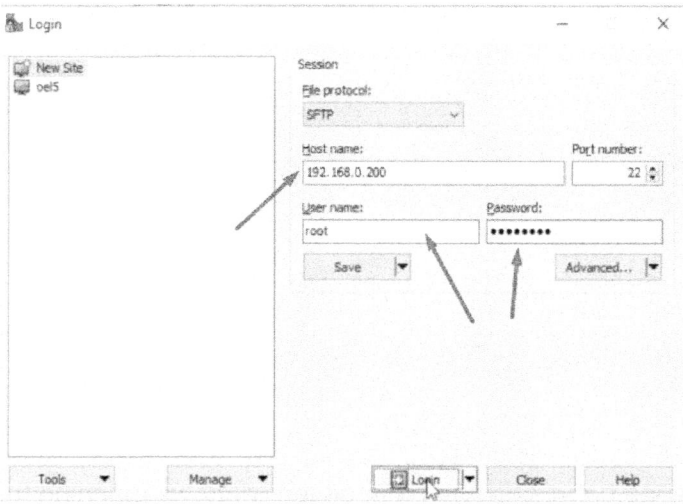

We will give the IP address, port number, username as root and the root password. Then click on Login.

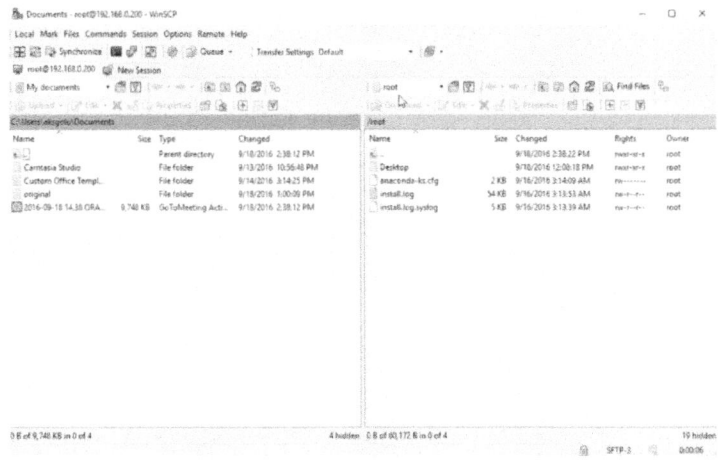

We can see our server folders on the right hand side.

When you go to the root mount point, you can see all the file systems from the Linux server.

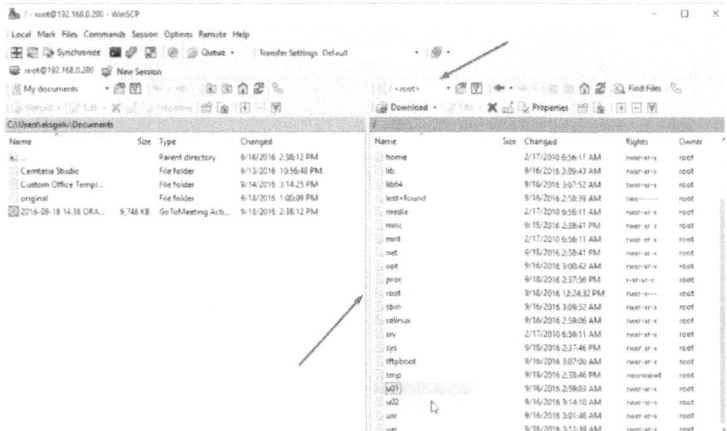

On the left hand side, we have all the windows machine folders.

Suppose you want to copy a file from windows to linux server. You just need to browse the file on left hand side and drag and drop to the location where you want to copy the file in your server.

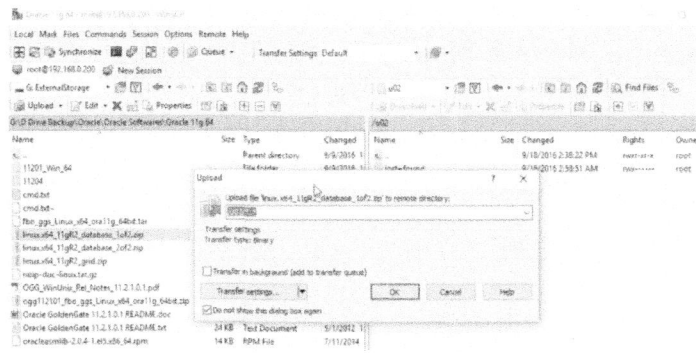

When you click on Ok, it will start copying the file.

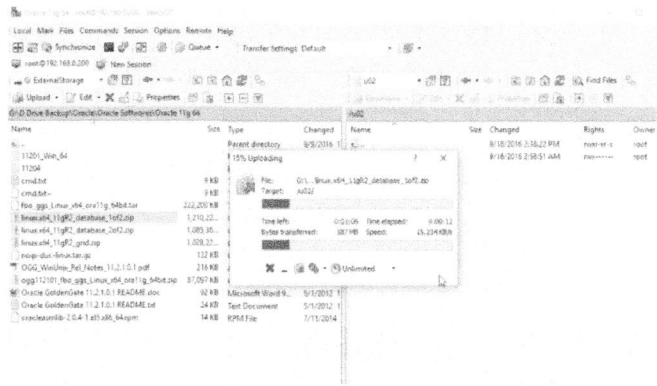

So, WinSCP is used to copy a file from your windows machine to your Linux server. If in case the Linux server is on different remote location also, you can use this tool in order to transfer the files.

Invoking Linux GUI on Windows

One big challenge as a DBA is when you try to install Oracle or when you try to invoke any graphical interface. PuTTY does not support graphical interface and also you do not have the option to login to the server as it is in a remote location or maybe the virtual machine for the server is created on to a different server.

In our case, we have the option to login to the GUI interface as our virtual machine resides on our own system. But in real time, you need to have some additional softwares in order to invoke the GUI interface.

When you use PuTTY, you need to install Xming software to invoke the graphical interface directly from PuTTY. So we will download the Xming software first.

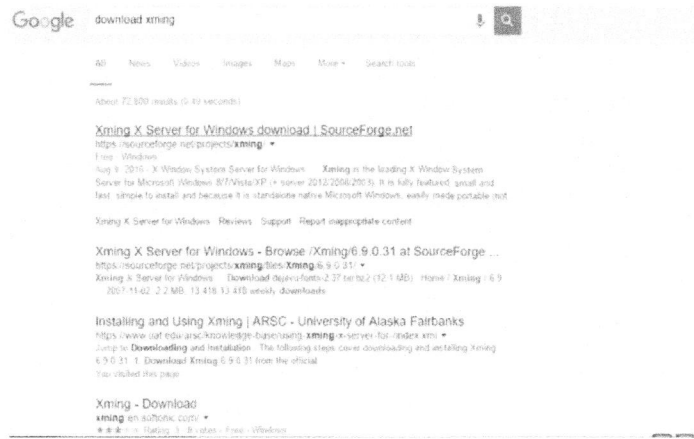

Type download Xming in google.com and click on the first result that we get.

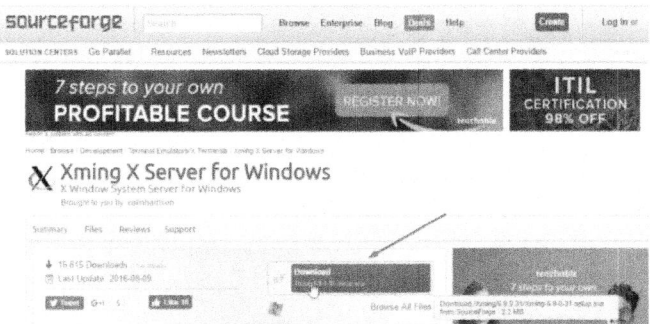

Then click on download. It will start downloading the software.

Once the download is completed, start the installer.

You can just go on clicking on Next for 3 to 4 screens. In between, it will ask you to create a desktop icon for Xming.

Then click on Install. It will start installing the software.

Finally click on Finish. There is not much to do in the installer. Once the installation is done, you can launch the software.

Xming is a small software like PuTTY. So before you try to invoke any graphical interface, make sure that you start Xming.

You just have to double click on the Xming icon and it will start in the system tray. You can see in your system tray that Xming is running.

There is one setting that we need to set in PuTTY to invoke the graphical user interface on your windows screen.

Open PuTTY and click on SSH option under the connection.

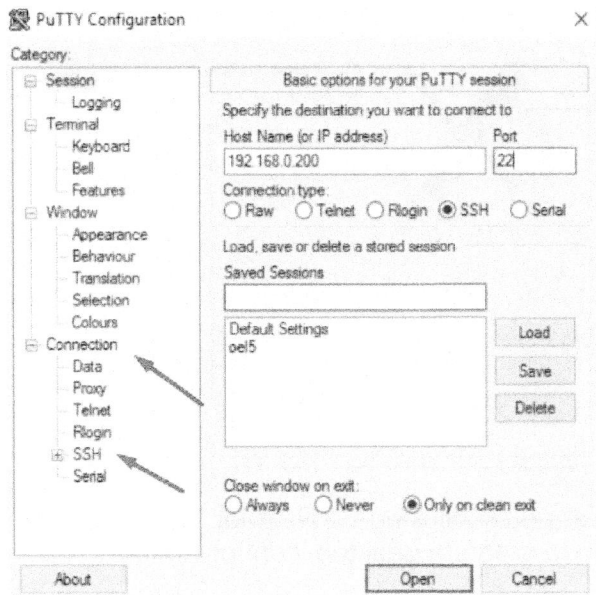

Then go to X11 option under SSH

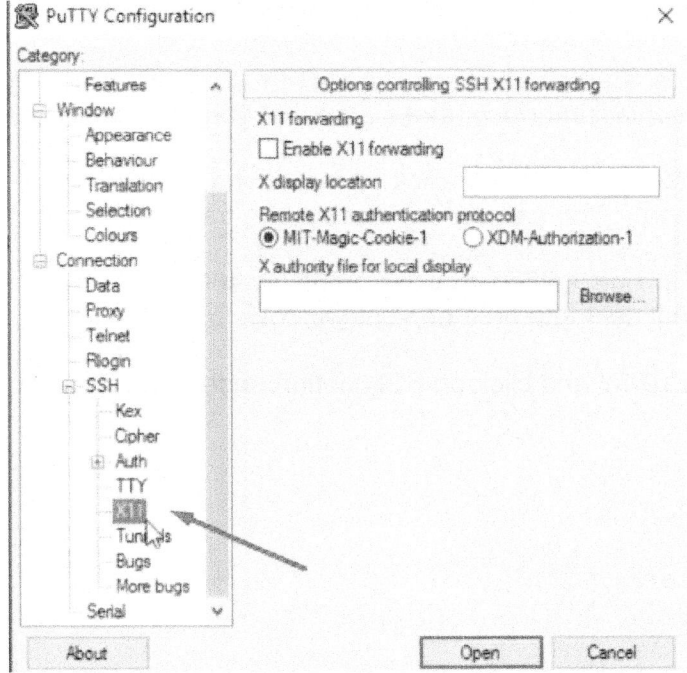

You need to enable X11 forwarding option here and then click on Open.

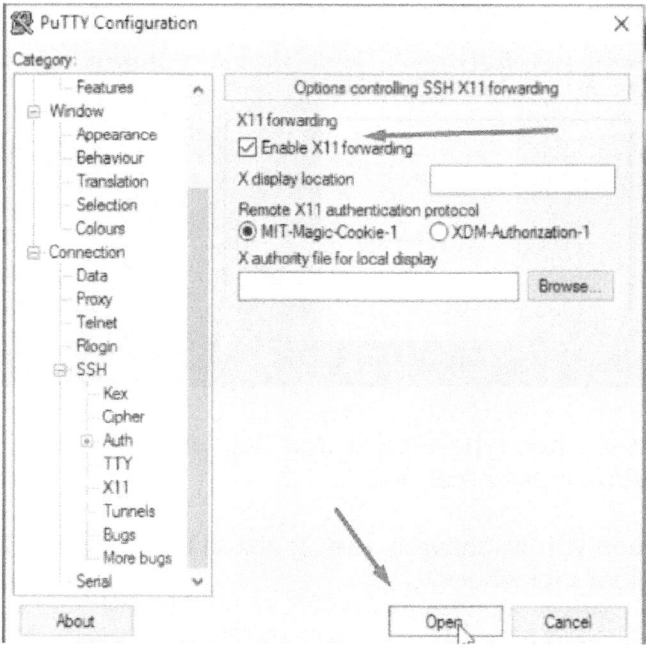

It will open a PuTTY session. Log in using root username and password.

Then type xclock

This is one way to test whether the GUI is working or not.

You will see that the Xclock from the Linux machine is displayed on the windows machine.

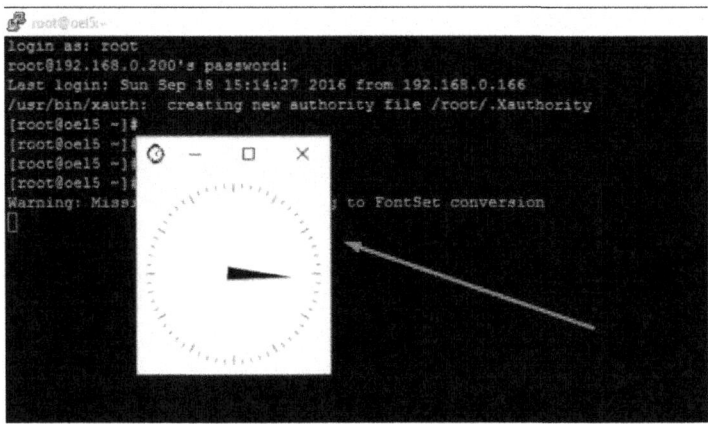

Similarly, we can type Firefox and see whether Firefox will start on our windows machine or not.

Sometimes you will have some issues in invoking the GUI interface. So how to troubleshoot?

- You need to check whether the Xming software is running in the system tray or taskbar or not.
- You need to check whether the X11 forwarding is enabled or not.

Important: The GUI interface will only work with the user with which you are connected. In the above case, it is the root user. If you switch to any other user (suppose oracle user) in the same session and then try to use the GUI. You will not be able to do so.
In order to use the GUI as an oracle user, you need to login to the PuTTY session using oracle username only.

Thankyou!

Your comments encourage us to produce quality content, please take a second and say 'Hi' to me and let me and my team know what you thought of the book … p.s. It would mean the world to me if you send a quick email to me ;)

Email: support@dbagenesis.com

- Link to full course: https://dbagenesis.com/
- Link to all DBA courses: https://dbagenesis.com/courses
- Link to real-time projects: https://dbagenesis.com/p/projects
- Link to support articles: https://support.dbagenesis.com

DBA Genesis provides all you need to build and manage effective Oracle technology learning. We designed DBA Genesis as a simple to use yet powerful online Oracle learning system for students. Each of our courses is taught by an expert instructor, and every course is available with a challenging project to push you out of your comfort zone!!

DBA Genesis is currently the fastest & the most engaging learning platforms for DBAs across the globe. Take your database administration skills to next level by enrolling into your first course.

Follow us on Social Media:

- Facebook: https://www.facebook.com/dbagenesis/
- Instagram: https://www.instagram.com/dbagenesis/
- Twitter: https://twitter.com/DbaGenesis
- Website: https://dbagenesis.com/
- Contact us: https://dbagenesis.com/p/contact

All the best and goodbye for now!

Arun Kumar

Notes

Printed in Great Britain
by Amazon

55339258R00108